FINISHING LINE PRESS
www.finishinglinepress.com

Soviets on Venus

poems by

Thomas E. Simmons

Finishing Line Press
Georgetown, Kentucky

Soviets on Venus

ISBN 979-8-88838-217-2 First Edition

Publisher: Leah Huete de Maines
Editor: Christen Kincaid
Illustrations by Yasemin Arkun
Cover Art: Paul Peterson—'Aeromotor Grey Painting'
Author Photo: Aaron C. Packard
Cover Design: Elizabeth Maines McCleavy

Order online: www.finishinglinepress.com
also available on amazon.com

Author inquiries and mail orders:
Finishing Line Press
P. O. Box 1626
Georgetown, Kentucky 40324
U. S. A.

Table of Contents

For Ethan,
who
helped me

Logos I

my
throne
was

in a
pillar
of
cloud

i
dwelt
in

the
highest
heavens

i
compassed
the vault

Sirach 24:4-5

An Anonymous Venera. Photograph by the Author.

Logos II

Let them compete in
showing obedience

to one
another

Rule of St. Benedict 72:6

Logos III

She is perceived by those who love her

Men watching for her at dawn
will not be disappointed

She will be found sitting at the gate
She makes her rounds

Wisdom 6:12-16

Logos IV

Whoever holds her
fast inherits
glory

Sirach 4:13

Pushkin's Duel (1837)

years after
the atheist Pushkin

wrote letters   of that which was:

Chiseled in white stone—

The buildings
topped with
fiery glory

A golden cross
on every dome—

he cramped   he lamented a spasm would divert him from climbing a staircase
his spleen was   a magnate   dousing his disposition with the worst kind of
merchandise   grimacing he spread   out   paper blankets and minted a
tantrum-complaint:

Troubles, grieves, agitation—

a soreness worried him   he'd misplaced pleasantness; he'd lost dignity and the
thick-necked Tsar couldn't be   blamed for all of it   but his brother-in-
law, French officer Georges-Charles de Heeckeren d'Anthès had   scandalized
Natalia so Pushkin could

blame him instead Pushkin shot him but the manly strumpet with chrome
barrels and whipped-cream hair had better aim   chiseling an opening in the
poet   a stenciled ideogram; tokens ashen on a dome a misshapen lettered
lozenge   lodged in Pushkin's lodge

Lead in him; in his hip   near the Black River   so much black lodged there; a
boy's leaden finless missile   a dented deformed blunted slug found   an
agreeable still place in him to froth;   memory lost   as stars nictated on—
Venus among them

Pushkin's Death (1837)

Pushkin lamented as she switched off again at day-break he broke he broke Pushkin couldn't bear it his whimpering mouth made a Venus shape there was a protracted day with more suffering and no progress at all the next night was as cloudy as Venus

the clouds above Pushkin closed ranks and obscured her, foretelling that Pushkin would expire, which he did Pushkin could do that he winked off but Venus was unperturbed by a black river-side end of him of Александр Сергеевич Пушкин she remained

unfazed by his dispatch her biceps were unmoved by it or by any of those watery poems she was wary of his laical stanzas her baptism unmoved by the poet or by his often tedious, seldom vicarial, & thoroughly unlyrical repeat-groans

Pushkin gone
his lips still wet they

met the end with this text:

The senseless body
It is indifferent
wherever it rots

he meant his own, his groans did they counseled a blotting of 184 years Pushkin's groans flooded his fuel pump they over-stuffed the flu-ash in the coal-flue they tried again now they cleared their throats and urged themselves by means of the lines

We must all go under the eternal vault
And someone's hour is already at hand

as an offering to the tomb already being cut and soon filled in o're them a finality with few gathered guests Natalia among them though the Tsar stayed away he kept low under layered bedcovers seeming to every crafty satellite like a freshly smoothed grave

Soviet Scientists *Canto 1*: Konstantin Tsiolkovsky

Scarlet fever infected the man
as a boy in Izhevskoye taking
most of his hearing / He turned
to books; 2 spherical trigonometry

Before 2 long, he had thoroughly
worked out Tsiolkovsky's Formula—

an elegant dynamite *whooosh!* of
a math for prosecuting stelae up—

Next, he penned more; calculating the
escape velocities required to evacuate
shrieking falsetto interplanetary trips
with rocket stages / one after another
after another slicing / double-barreled
zefir-parallels of wrapped, bundled,
sequenced tendons; like train engines —spent—

dropping away; potsherds-footage;
relayed-ballets of his career steps;
his investigations ending when the
Bolsheviks granted him a pension…

He died in 1935 as someone let loose
of the other end of his life-kite string —spent—

dropping away; he exited the scene
but his formula refused to; instead

it gave birth to scores
of lady rocket ships—
one after another
after another

Like an Accentual Metre March

Celestial frames of reference marches
verticalness to this aslant-of-worlds
stomping upon axes spun 'round Plato
"I'm not here in the same way that they're there,"
One could cry, eye-spying Perelandra
They'd look up; away from philosophy
But one who sees, goes out—over—into
If there is breeze—if we are made of air—
We lack amiability planted
there a-sipping disorientation
since *they* would be *standing*, just plumb; upright
While we—found in a valley, here—*we pitch*
All this is hinted in the synoptics
Triple it gazing through angstrom optics

Soviet Scientists *Canto 2*: Yuriy Vasilievich Kondratyuk

A dishy dark-pupiled Ukrainian:
Олександр Гнатович Шаргей
His mother married his pater in January
and Yuri infiltrated the world that June

She taught French in Kiev; a social
activist, thus, she was declared insane
His great-grandfather had battled Napoleon
His father loved physics. Yuri read his books.

While fighting on WWI's Caucasian Front, Yuri
filled notebooks with ideas like 'Kondratyuk's Loop'
which reckoned trajectories for orbit rendezvous—for
mastering an orbit, then promoting ones to better them

selves as on a rilled turntable a needle jumped over
strains of Shastakovich's 'To October' to inspire
Yuri to design a massive wooden grain elevator
without a single nail—and to name it 'Mastodon'

Nails were few—Mastodon's construction was clever
but construed as a subversion—it was without nails!
But a 13,000-ton Siberian elevator sans nails must be
designed to collapse, blockhead-bureaucrats figured

So the NKVD labeled him a saboteur and off
Yuri went to spend three years gutted in the gulag
Later, in *Conquest of Interplanetary Space* (1925),
he explicated the gravitational-slingshot-technique

He also authored *To Those Who Would Read when*
Building (a spacecraft) earlier; it went unpublished
The title might suggest that not everyone who
built would undertake first to *read* (as he had)

That only the select would read when building—
That it was for *those* that the book was intended

He volunteered for the Red Army in 1941
Nazis shot him dead while fixing a cable

Oleksandr Ignatyevich Shargei was his *real* name;
Yuriy Kondratyuk was an identity he had *assumed*
The first Yuriy Kondratyuk was a student at Kiev
University who had died of tuberculosis in 1921

Oleksandr had been conscripted into the White
Army at age 25, the penalty for which was death
Accordingly, he became Yuriy Kondratyuk instead
becoming a misplaced student who had died of TB

carrying on as if nothing had happened living secretly
while in plain view. Once he'd fluttered from them—
he'd run for Poland, but he was nabbed at the border—
& allowed to escape only because he looked deathly

So 'Deathly' had escaped execution by erecting alternative
identities but a Nazi bullet ensured an end to his deceptions
He fell forward—Oleksandr Shargei; Yuriy Kondratyuk—
the cable fell from his grasp; he tried to stand; he couldn't

The Kamen-na-Obi granary: largest in the world, it
no longer stands either, but not for want of nails
Both it and its maker crushed themselves out

Soviet Scientists *Canto* 3: Gavriil Adrianovich Tikhov

This Belarusian
used chromatic aberration
to decidedly stair-maze an
unfeathering of spectrographs
for the surface sobbed ruffles of
the mirth with which he would flirt

He ascended in a gelatin balloon to elbow
meteors with his friends from the Sorbonne
Sternly clutched by the puffs, he was, as the
blue-gas-flame sibilated girlishly for buoyancy
'He fell for the falling stars,' his friends chuckled

But the title of his autobiography—
Sixty Years at the Telescope—would
sum up most of his days at the office

He extracted sly spectra from leaves
Zestily, he extrapolated from them
He'd rail against mean geocentrism

He wrote *Astrobotany* and
he postulated; he prospected

He splashed—and he asked—
Is There Life on Other Planets?

Ogling through his Maksutov meniscus
squinting to discern pale details beyond
the charisms he practiced, what he could

make out were her colors, and so based on
them—and what he knew of Earth's plants
he would locate a grand blue herbage garth

on her—there! upon her Fallopians
just underneath her unmentionables

Illus. 1

Soviet Scientists *Canto 3.5:* Tikhov in Awkward Rhyme

Shallow oceans for the sailing
Temperatures benign at best
Through the scope tube's lens
Venus invited tropical whaling

Ol' Tikhov sketched that which the probes
would find—with a quick & chary math he
Predicted a nursemaid covered in plants
Waggish blue stolons on clear flushing lobes

Later, people laughed at those precepts
But never his wife, Ludmila Popova
Diminutive? Yes, but just a hop over
From his side, sketching a sky, she is

She knows what is true, robust, & upright
To silence the agitators (& Tikhov as well)
She can fix cauldrons of notions to tell
Tightening scope, key blue buds alight

Mind Them

Fancy: All the tall bright loyalists
arrayed in formation; 6 deep &
5 abreast buzzing excitement
but perfectly composed &
with crackerjack postures
toed-in toward 1-another

This platoon of elegance
is swathed in discipline
Finger-stitched; proud
smart-alecky stone
affixed to trellises
saucily sprouting
fences as trestles
an amethyst
program—
Skene's
glands

No, nothing about these
fine limbs is titillating,
provocative, or grit-strewn
They stand without sandals
and the smoke about their
exposed ankles is sluggish

They are resolute laborers
in the vineyard dedicated
to the means of production
They are armored anchorites—
on whose tonsures is engraved
in a sans serif font, "here we are"

They are femme fatales
only to diminished rivals
They trifle with no one
Flinch at no thing and yes

all were pre-wed to a mantle
as each knew of whose body

they were members; they were
winged beating virgos intacta
in the catacombs preferring
His space light to grottos; dark;
specked; fluttering wings flutter-
ing; singed petticoats shuttering

to Tarshish, Pud, and Lud—
which will draw the bow—
to Tubal, then, and Javan
to the recall-coastlands
winging a single-track
& not any path-to-death

The waterless sea parted; a sure
artery for their horses; their
hooves led to the lowest star
No middle ground opened
to objects of a perception
They penciled out conceit

Messages came from Theman;
The holy one from the mountain
O' Pharan was obliging to them
With the trunks of palms
they scattered the proud
with the strength of arms

Their scrutiny? Rays
shining from hidden
rifts in rakish rocks
Kinfolk. Strength:
an orange-juiced
pleasantry; a fair
spatial surprise

2MV-1 No. 1: Smokey & the Bandwidth

Perceive: 1962. Their sieve lantern—
She ushers herself toward a sponged
celibate tryst with a curled ascetic sand

Her attention—snapping to / Her mystical rivets—flush
Her suit—just-so & principled / Yet—she mis-carried
& before they came to understand—*tut-tut-tut...*
          that she'd burned up—scuppered—
          scorched—left off—failed—nixed—died
there must have been proper hushed
pursed sweaty orisons—querulousness seepings
through folded hands / triangle-d like hi-steeples
with pine-pews, folded paper, and paper necks stuck
between finger joints which were no longer hers to join

even if devotions weren't strictly permitted
to all the scientists, engineers, and toilers, nor
to the virgins, nor the Stavrophores, nor a genus, really; 2 no one

else; the orthodox cathedrals
were quiet with a space with-
in them as vast as *any* space

Even if the interiors of the cathedrals
were decapulated of all worshippers

Even if the worshippers stayed away
and all the icons were ignored, still

there would have been demands;
whispered anxieties to our lady—

concentric rings of pious salutations to our
Theotokos—essential generations straining
before a vaporization of unspun-cylinder's

Dei-Genitrix science-ministry was known

Tyzhuli Sputnik or "Sputnik 7" · *I*

The ordinary air unlatched
her armor into meat-kernels
as she (also) spat-screamed
The 'air' part was ordinary
Her 'armor' part was well-
coated; *business*-plated but

since it was late, no one noticed—
(much as them doctors miss
their alb's cancer; just crossly
un-penciling it from charts) but
surely it had been there—while
she suds-showered and studied and

two years later a boy stubbed
his toe on her and announced
everything as if he had won it...
the first part was predictable—
but only after defeat was beheld
—the second part was just an improbable

way to re-jigger a malfunction
as a *ptasie mleczko* confectionary; a
gas-car-crash as a trilobite-meringue *thud*

debriding the slough
off her bruised kits
under a bruised sky

pollarding her without
snarling without even
withdrawing without

a distress in the whole world
buried near an urn-dun shore
Mourners starry-eyed, they cried

II (Breakfast at Stringencies)

for some moments, she was just wished and awash
in the speckled cry of a burgundy velocity

but her striations cracked
it cracked
she cracked
open
she cracked open-less

her back opened less as an unplucked Russian azalea than as a
combustible *vatrushka*—that is, all at once

what happened was a cracking as unmannered as it was
mordantly minatory

what happened were weighty ribs with a longstanding and
thoroughly disordered Stalinist repression

what happened was that her heart-shaped PT-200 transformer
short-changed its arterial current, so a diseased timer never rang
its squilla bell, which caused the svelte (but silenced) metal-
clappered-hand to fail to issue its command to ignite her modest
4th-stage block L

and thus, her gloves quickly singed right down to her chasuble

and consequently, the carriage couldn't muster ambition even for
the next parish

first, it balked and then it whumped her rachis (as she insisted in
an astral mud, chugging from a vulgar position) limbs akimbo

revolution-to-revolution, she'd hawk on about it for 40 ellipses,
coughing once at each turn, wallpaper-patterning her demise, but

after 40, her catheter withdrew and the last of her reverie was
whisperingly pinched out of Her in all of His white empty space

III (My Life as a Dog)

Surreptitiously unlading the stainless-steel
autopsy table wasn't the same as rinsing it
The Soviets bungled her launch plan while
the West made a hash of her search patties

Required to tap-report satellite unbucklings
an oscine misconstrued her autopsy away by
claiming the abbess—outfitted with a neat
buoyant globe-float habit designed for rid-

ing imagined briny-reservoirs in style—was
truly a sober heavy-barque riding combers
Meanwhile, two Italian brothers were skep-
tical—*so* skeptical (in fact) that they managed

to reconstitute muffled cosmonaut heartbeats
transmitted by the tug-seiner-nun's radio—
So *certain* were they that a doomed Russian
had faced a space-death just as Laika had in her

three-point dog-harness in 1957 (when her
sputnica's R-7 sustainer congested its own
catarrh) that they discerned phantom heartbeats
from the static of Pleiades and it wasn't the last

cosmonaut heartbeat they took note of which
didn't pump blood (or bile) as over 4 years
'they wiped out an entire squad of fictitious
cosmonauts,' explained one space historian

whose grin-muscles only partially suppressed
themselves in the ironic transmission of these
little-known, little-acknowledged, half-tubered
typewriter etchings—and so much the better for her

IV (After Math)

22 days after her launch,
Traveler-Cat came back
home; to Siberia, in fact,
plopping cloth some-
where, as gravity super-
ceded her stair-climbing;

Two years after that, her
iridescence was mostly
hidden cables ringing;

Two years after *that,* a
roving boy came across
her charred remains near
the Baryusha River
(including contorted
pennants celebrating
(falsely) her big trip)

which the young patriot
dredged out from gravel
& delivered to KGB men

Pennants sang dirges
which the boy scooped
up from the petrichor-
smelling grasses & mud,
grinning from ear to ear—
Iridescent he; as if he'd just
won back his dearest pet

But Venus has no oceans &
Tyzhuli Sputnik never had
a heartbeat, so, afterwards,
she'd spin her lathe in a dim,
clay KGB office, unobserved

Illus. 2

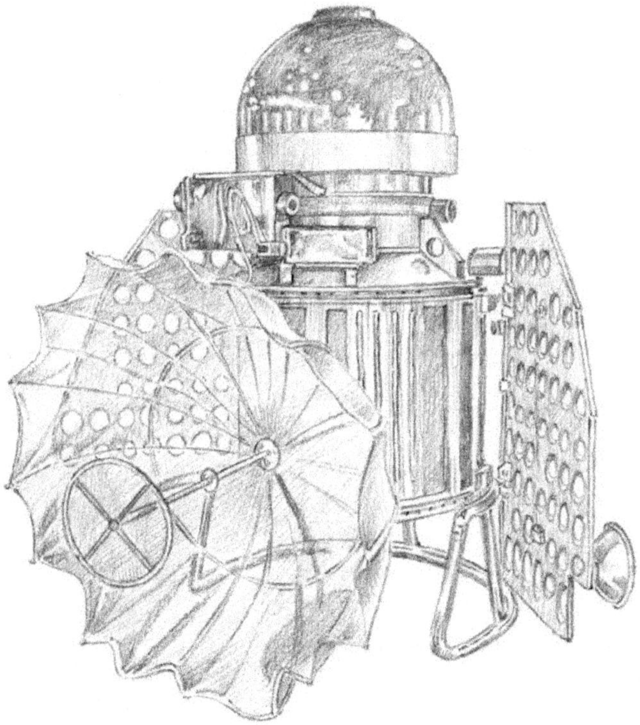

a star is born: Venera-1

This one is a very tall dryad
with a cornflower domed top hat
festooned with parabolic antennas
Her name tag dismantles something sad

Венера-1 is our sly steampunk weathercock
with a pair of lavish ion traps with which to
seize handfuls of unwitting, impressionable ions
—catch and release—while her defective sylph—
Tyzahely Sputnik—has tightened up the strictures

Her stillborn sister hawked in her hedgerow
Never left her launch pad; just issued a single
declaration-concussion before spittle-stalling

But this pillarist took wing—embellishing

powering her ullage engine up—up
up to a waxy plasma hierarchy there

she surveyed unknown stone-breezes
and announced them before fizzling to
a climax zenithing across a radio telescope
(which may have detected some so faintly
fragrant signals of her in June but she'd
stopped radio-whispering
back long before then)

Perhaps her solar
detection sensor
overheated—

Melted her in the maw
impossible distances
from her tidy home

Venera-2 (or 'Roadtrip' in 2 flats)

Lady mechanics called her 'something else'
She'd set her ambitions on this spiral scent
She'd eye-lash through our cloud napkins
Gather potency in her endowed hatpin,
chord-propel into a humble heliocentric,
and then wait, traversing the length

of the span between eight doctrines …
& within four months she'd arrived
She levelled th' bellows; tweaked
her yaw; adjusted her ornaments
and readied herself for a flyby
Radio contact was cut so that

all of her needled instruments
could flush full-*on* at once and
she'd shift her attentions to them
bending brisk across the Tuesday
Then, once she'd swept the parade,
she could switch the instruments *off*

again to radio back her diary entries
She was executing a *grande jeté*
tens quicker than 1600 jet pilots
when first one hiccup and then
another crinkled concentration
initially just a minor short but

when her radiator failed her it
didn't make even a hiss-growl
(although it bellied her up just the
same) She was hit below the water-
line and capsized just like the Moskva
Even her cuticles melted cleanly away

Burnt Birds and Flowers

Surround: This eremite
at a farther semidiameter
on the Kazakhstan plain,
you xenomorphs of a redscale fauna

a far meadow of larkspur and rows of monks'
hood, of buttercups, vetch, and rotating clover
of fireweed, of foxglove, watched over by bustards

But the launch site has been
scrubbed clean of the natural world
excepting a few remaining
dandelions and blue-cheeked bee-eaters

The dandelions swab in the pavement cracks
despite the best efforts of the groundskeepers

The hungry bee-eaters gell and warble
with a persistence of like magnitude

The Baikonur launch site has the aspect
of a large table set with two showcased dead
life forms—both tall constructs: a launch tower
and she—a gasping who is *so anxious* to succor

an outrageous furnace
with neck-snapping zephyrs
to read Dante so earnestly &
to spur on gold in the furnace:
"A block of fiery porphyry"

that no one notices the songbirds enciphering
her, sculpting an imagined maypole 'round
the she-missile—their flight unsurpassed
until lift-off when at the appointed hour
the crowds set and the larks pronounce:

Три *(Three)* Два *(Two)* Один *(One)*

When My17-year-old Left Home for Brown

A slouched count-down completed whereupon
a harp string inflorescence gently distended from
beneath her hoops, extinguishing every dandelion—
scattering all songbirds and some pollen like crumbs

She had pined for that tick-command
which would send her into the welkin
toward the tan damsel, whose appeal
lacked even a single gram of fecundity

We might advance, 'she is like the inside
of an oven,' but for the suggestion that
we might find a cake in there baking

But it was this to which her allocations
yearned toward; a not-unpleasant ache

Ten thousand hogsheads of rich jam
in her stomach paused like a gravid
thick wound spring, thick as a trunk

She held fast to discipline and to the
practiced art she would bring to it all
Her manners would not be thwarted
She suspired to serve those men on the steppes

Upon her timed culmination, she would clear
the tabletop with a single gesture—hexing the
sugared dandelions into burnt French fry stubs

displacing all of the pipits—showering pretend
hoar-frost generously; like some ash or confetti
murmuring: *blackberry, blackberry, blackberry*

NyQuil® So-You-Can-Rest-Medicine

Not an absent-minded one
No mere pelvis-plaint
Her immaterial
self was an aperture to
what was sown & unromantic

Her joints needed no slaking of
greasing with their precision
for tolerances—
with their tolerance for precisions—
She humbly tooled brittle poise

Before her: Theophany
Her heart? Steadfast
Vindication: Her rear guard
Still, far chimes of distraction
opposed her throughout her trip

Her trail was cold but not gone
It had not gone cold
She tried ignoring the
examinations piled into her
and the banjos in her armpits

Star shapes from some fugue beast
from the clean abyss: a few
lodged in her thorax
As she coughed, they emitted—
And with that, her melancholy lifted

Geography Lesson

Next: A field trip to Kosmodrom Baykonur's
launch center in southern Kazakhstan's
desert steppe where horse-winds comfort
or distress depending on their bridleways

Perhaps the name Kosmodrom Baykonur
was selected to deceive the Western Bloc by
telegraphing its location 320 kilometers northeast
(to a mining town of that name) of its true location

but the cresentoid-shaped spaceport near
Leninsk isn't really lost, it's east of the
Aral Sea, north of the Syr Darya River

surrounded by plains which please
the radio signals and their démodé
preferences for uninterrupted spaces

near the equator which endows greater
velocity into the ICBMs to-be-launched
from the waist of a spinning-earth where

Afanasiy Ilich Tobonov found paths of
mass wildlife deaths exactly drawn on
flight paths of the wind-borne rockets

Not more than a few centuries previous,
wild horses would have consumed grasses
jubilantly and not more than a decade or so

previous, deer romped about more or less
jubilantly in the same proximities until
the rockets became increasingly somatic

Deer had been incinerated and the
people of Eliptyan became cancerous
from the rocket fuel. So did Tobonov.

Those deaths and their causes:
another series of lost things—

Lost in the way people die
unjustly and stay that way

Kosmodrom Baykonur was lost in the
way obscured things are lost; the wild
horse herds were lost in another way

but the spilled rocket fuel wasn't lost

at all
it found its way
into arteries & bones

And as our field trip scuttles back to school
we'll pass fields of spent launch equipment
which the local population salvages thereby
spilling more fuel where it doesn't belong

A Leninsk Mother's Prayer (1965)

Inkar, you stiffen but
do not straighten as
you walk to school

Too much sunshine
perhaps; a sun too
close—or just not
enough milk in you

some things do come
too close and a danger
can be registered so

blink away the red-
ness in your eyes and
arrange yourself

remember your
father who died in
the Nedelin disaster

remember every October 24th—a date
dangerously close to November 7th—
the Bolshevik Revolution birthday

All our men incinerated
running from a fireball
stopped by the fence
and quickly overtaken

or brittled by the
toxic missile fuel
component vapors

They were too close—
Perhaps you are
too near—playing

with your classmates
in the bilious grasses while
I scavenge for sharp bits there

with the other widows
those who remain
still above ground

sharpened themselves
Some say there's an-
other poison here, but

A little more rest,
A prayer, some milk;
You'll straighten up

Kosmos-21

She whom Americans call 'Cosmos 21' aviated from Kosmodrom Baykonur on (American) Veteran's Day, 1961.

Everything was conducted in whispers. She blanketed secretly from the Soviet concealed location of Kosmodrom Baykonur which enjoyed particularly florid-orange sunsets. Sunsets painted over lantern glass silhouetted the birch-ribbed launch towers pounded into the hard-packed ground which smelled of gasoline, worm husks, and body odor. Against the tiger lily roofed cavity, she was also silhouetted, too; a silkworm worrier.

She ascended as if she was extracting meaning from the noctilucent dark-centered streaks with each stage. Each stage tumbled away from her like discarded prom dates when she was through with them.

While the name Космодро́м Байкону́р may have been selected for deception, she was no impaneled ambulance doting on secrecy. She was concerned with staying aloft and delivering her grade school patient who gobbled solid fuel intravenously like potato chips. She brewed a black tea from Odessa and packed it into his dressing. She monitored his fuel pressure twice each hour with a nylon cuff and a laminae gauge. She was assiduous about everything. Her corrugated brow never uncrinkled.

(At the same time, she was nationalistic to a fault and shirked individualism in all its commercially available varieties. She cared deeply for dignity and was ignorant of autonomy.)

She amplified herself through the mesosphere. Then, fully primed, she careened around, gathering an impressive momentum, and for a time, all seemed ordered, but her orbit began to rot black oil from the inside; it decayed first slightly, and then more noticeably.

She leaked. Her orbit became a lullaby being sung more and more out of tune, with more and more words mispronounced and notes slurred. Her tuning fork ally faded into the greenish fog. She was losing her way. She was so sparagmatized.

She could no longer recall her favorite Bible verse. Her prayer cards became all jumbled up with her operating manual pages as if a deck had been shuffled. Then the orbit itself began to slur. Without even any coaching from the jar of horsehead bow operettas at her disposal, her notes all became sharp.

Three days later, she flatlined. We're not even sure whether she was meant to attempt a flyby canticle or not. She'd been as shrouded in Soviet secrecy as her launch site. Perhaps they've forgotten her altogether. Any descorts stifled in her windpipe would be by now, in all likelihood, irretrievable.

Secrecy mixed with forgetfulness does that to a girl. It's a beet and potato casserole worth forgetting.

Maybe she was intended from the beginning to remain in a geocentric orbit—a 'parking orbit'—which makes it sound pedestrian—it makes *her* sound pedestrian— but a polished metal handiwork with gemstone sirens carried by her own velocity and spinning through a space of professed beauty, tethered only by the hardscrabble gravity of us, is far from pedestrian—she was a tether.

She was a tether ready to *snap*!

Snap, she did.

Her axles crescendo-squealed before locking, steam escaping from various cracks in her personhood. The squeal escaped her like a swallow from a tea kettle and lengthened into a crow's foot lariat stretched beyond its test limits. Like a sprinkler connected to a hose of vaporized puss, the holes in her calves spouted her safety nets. They threw her lifeboats away even as she began composing a song to keep them attentive. The lifeboats departed in a flock, headed in the direction of the Trifid Nebula.

Soon, her skin began to buckle. Her creaking chart read like the Atlas Mountains, blipping:

> *v*'s after *v*'s after *v*'s.
>
> Then *V*'s after *V*'s after *V*'s.
>
> Then six lower-case *w*'s.

Then a tracing of the tail of a *g*.

Slower.

And the fading spark-sound of an *s*.

Stopping.

Her hair falling out. Her locks threshed. Her thatch annulled. Soon, her scalp looked plucked.

Her patient was excavated to lighten her load, tumbling out of her, all to no avail. The windowsill portal collapsed upon her. Her feck was just a speck.

Soon, she was on life-support. Nothing beeped to announce it.

The only doctors who put direct pressure on her avulsion and tried to find a pulse were not medically trained. Her torch was reduced to a bouquet of acceptance as to what would happen next.

And then what would happen next happened:

She stalled, lessening, punctured her spectators' rotary phone rinds, dialed in the inevitable, and came back hot.

Conspiring only with herself, she burned down to the shape of one ghost—shaped ash piece.

Crusty. Too lengthy now. Bending. Leaning beyond her center of gravity.

She was an obsolete precipice. Her tip toppled off right at the filter. She was smudged out; incapable of being re-lit for another drag.

She had been reduced to a metaphor.

Illus. 3

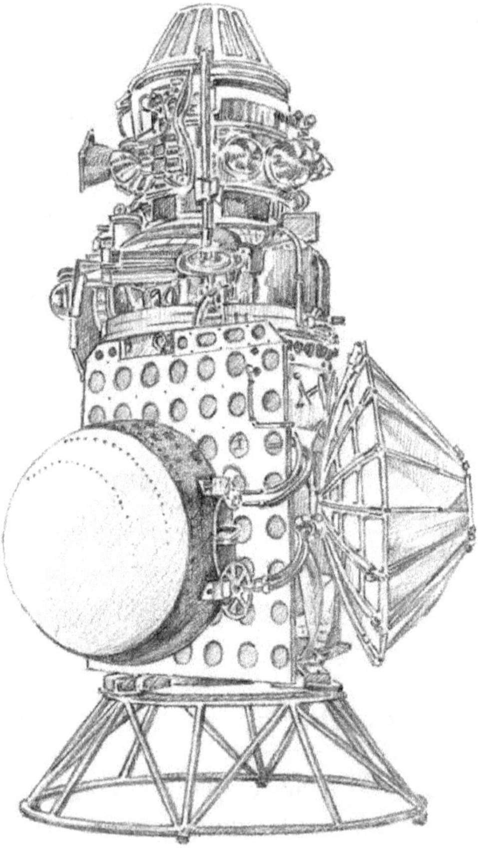

V-3

That spring, the young exegete crashed; purpled herself across a dead bocage of extraterrestrial mire with the proud medallions and Soviet Coats of Arms clipped to her lapels, while back home they made a wearisome postage stamp in her honor; to 'stamp her with honor' some said, in red and grey, and thereby modestly credit her as a heroine; a martyr; the first smelt craft to reach the surface of another planet, and rather dramatically at that.

The assembled bureaucrats claimed credit and sang songs of achievement. Their collective pitch left something to be desired.

There wasn't much left of her semiosis (or of the medallions (or the Coats of Arms, either, for that matter)) given her speed of impact, except that honor.

It wasn't what you'd call a soft landing. She became ejecta, toppling all over herself.

But before that, with her long passage across the gargoyle's shawl behind her, she'd aimed herself steadily at her target.

She situated the vector of the second orbit in her crosshairs.

On her first attempt, her trajectory had been unfaithful to her and she'd bypassed the ragged fur of the outer atmosphere by sixty thousand kilometers or so, but the communists pulled some levers and spun some wheels and sloppily programmed a corrective maneuver into her temples, ramming her into the planet, they say, on the first of March.

From a ravine back home came the tuneless singing. The banal praises.

And within that singing and labyrinth of human motivations which powered her could be found ambition, allegiance, a clove or two of fealty, and some sizable cravings for creation-revelation fixes, but there was a germ in the petri dish, a minotaur in the riddle, a basilisk in the nursery, against which she lacked any immunity because, you see, contemporary outer space historians have concluded (more or less in concert; a dissonant concert-choir of lovable, nerdy men who disdain contact lenses for reasons no one can identify) that the new soviets actually lost her in the cusp of her flight in mid-April—when she scalped—and that she never exuded upon a curve at all and—as a result—was devoured sideways (by dishonesty and dissembling, rather than via a heroic mashing) and that if she did (perish prematurely in a bellow of propaganda, as now seems the case), she may never be truly credited; her honor thereby discredited, except for the official and wholly unattractive postage stamp bearing her fissures which even the most dedicated communist-friendly philatelists deride for its nested-homeliness; its hollow-headedness in recalling the youth's deeds (if she achieved them, which we'll likely never know) and a split-abdomen of slumping reflected upon a cancelled stamp and the medals rudely sutured to her before she'd taken her leave.

Such was the journey of V-3.

1 Nurse Named 3

Journeys require propellants. One sort or another.
Peppered meats for mountain hikes
Cigarettes rolled for deacons
Wood matches for rockets
Search-notes for gospels
A full teat for a babe
Ash for cinders
Bras for teens
A cross 4 us
Commands
Sanctity
Liturgy
Willed
Desire
Water
Bread
Spirit
Wine
Dust
God
Us
V-
3

Venera-4 for 2

'Venera 4 split the Venusian sky in two'
a Russian girl might have pronounced this on
a Russian school playground to her best friend:
'Венера 4 раскололо венецианское небо надвое'

Venera 4 split the Venusian sky in two—We don't
know, but a true schoolgirl may have. In this play
ground one did—in what was then Leninsk
She crushed equations like Lenin strangled

Anastasia—that is, she had a flair for it—
She was not one for hopscotch or *koshki i*
myshki, except when she was the cat that
might lend her beauty to the inmost mice

Ringed with strength; that of disarmament
She didn't know her own strength or the
lack of poetic protein filaments in her
classmates, and so when she articulated

that simple line, gazing skyward, up, imaging
a mythic girdle, she failed to notice the gaping
'o' mouth of Svetlana, her comrade boon, age
ten, which her benign declaration had produced

A Certain Spacecraft Named Rapture

I would have stayed at my bench
and never ventured to lofty wheels
She extended some form of a hand
and asked me, 'Do you wish to scrub
lamellae in the water?' wrenching my
hand roughly, torqueing my shoulder

Her elbows were
damp & immutable
She yanked me—
not to the nearby
pool of water where
there might be fishes—
whose gills could take in
& let out—but upwards we leapt

We leapt like calves from modest stalls
What appeared to be loins were tenants
without the appearance of any thatching

After a time, she still held; she
took me by a lock of my head
to the entrance of the gateway
of the inner court that faces north
My throat was sore; my
arm consecutively numb
I'd ceased even to shiver

Silver scales
blanketed every
unzipped abundance
Scales which—seemingly
had fallen from her eyes
We dug through the wall
There was a single nostril

It was imbricated, just as she had promised

Coming-of-Age in No-Man's-Land

Para-Chimera met Sara-Mascara at the
Starbucks® precisely at 8:00 as agreed

& the first words from
her mouth yielded this:

> 'Venera 4 splendidly split Venusian skies' and rocket-wise,
> *everyone* noticed her. Everyone named her beautiful things
> since she was. Other languages have their words for Venus—
>
> *Tawera* (in Maori) *Nahid* (in Persian) *Morongo* (in
> Makoni) *Ngyandu* (in Swahili) *Ta'urua* (in Tahitan)
> *Kumanyefie* (in Ewe) *Vesper* (in Latin) *Lusaber* (in Ar-
> menian), *Tan-yondozo* (in Bashkir) *Vénus en français*
>
> Her atmosphere was scratched by a tall-cool-one!
> Tornado-like vortices yanked #4 against her poles
> as 'Venera the 4th split her sky in twain, polishing'

Para-Chimea paused
catching her breath

Sara-Mascara shrugged
unconcerned &
gestured to her Vespa

'probably just nerves'
she thought to herself

Runway Model Rocketry

She caromed. She zipped
A throaty turpentine voice

relayed unbiodegradable
fitly reproved enigmas &

it did so at just the right pace
neither rushed nor plodding

Not 'quick as a limpet' but
'as nimble as a pantomime'

Hitting the right spots, she
dabbed on her pulse points

her perfumed solvents; her
convoluted trails of exhaust—

pointing her pistols, she
grabbed life by the tonsils

She modeled Kondratyuk's loop
An introvert with an abacas skirt

She combed for a magnetic field
and detected brick-lined cenacles

She inverted the 8 histogram-jeweled
broad place gradients of another altar

Her object—so long named—was
now being refashioned; now vowing

Her 'amber sky sever-rived'   *[applause]*

A 'perforated performance'   *[curtain]*

Giovanni Domenico Cassini

Now admittedly, this 17th century astronomer once—sleep-deprived & squinting so hard that rose-moles stippled his chin—

'found' a moon teasing a kidney-shaped Venus and named it 'Neith'—goddess of Red Crown; war; inventor of weaving

& others confirmed his find, but they were all mistaken; she's moonless; a missing halo, vandalized; her clouds, reflective

Gossipers claim she once had a friend, but that an impact reversed both spins so lustily & brutishly that their velocities

were uncranked; retooled; reversed—which caused the friend who wasn't Neith to feral-corkscrew inward

Spiral-siphoned; lightened; their masses collided—orb & pal—recoiling; compressed salpicon; loudly crunched they melded

Earlier, others may have been rebuffed by her in the same way—like placenta; she does not appreciate

companions who circle her; doesn't suffer paramours gladly. It's hard to make friends like that—with friends like that, who needs

para-moons, but I know one who once paid her a visit. They would exchange gifts; find rapport. They touched woodcuts

hers was a myth in the making

Out here—an encyclopedia of glory
of swellings and forests and geysers

She had lent herself to the effulgent flyby temple
at zero percent interest and not a dram of collateral

Her reflectivity would impart unwavering parallax path-
ways and the cheers of all her parsimonious country[men]

Her breastbone throbbed but not from lack of celestial
methane. She recited a festal telemetry, constellating

'Everything that goes around comes around,' she smiled
to herself, squinting on account of the cosmic dust motes

Dialing in her latticed aim on a skeletal nebula off star-
board she began renaming everything one-by-one-by-one

Rounding the doorway, the curtains dot-illuminated them-
selves so she could coast the rest of the way on the breezes

Magnetic formulas & flowery morsels circumscribed specks embedded
with authenticities lacking day-to-night footsteps

Back there were neckline-kvells and equinoxes
Out here she could bisect, swim, trot, and carol

Out here, nothing was chaotic, nor grisly
Nothing was profane, nor crass, nor base

Nothing was higgledy-piggledy or unkempt
Nothing was whiskered or preened or sick

Out here, she was encyclopedias of glory
and her heart spooned her lungs each night

Without lies there were no transgressions
Not one cliché dangled from her bowels

Out here, she steered a marvelous vocation
with the grip of half a continent upon her

of swellings and forests and geysers
of episcopal networks & commitment

Illus. 4

Radar Ships on the Sea

The springtime tracking fleet—painted white, sleek, lustrous—chugged through the Black Sea, marching across the waves, outfitted with bulging beacons; fresh electronics; futuristic losses

Staffed with sailors swelling, tossed to and fro on the decks; there on the decks: hundreds of colicky edible stick-figures manifesting manliness in their store-bought pleated wool navy Japanese schoolgirl uniforms, tip toeing on greed-cornices

That greediness—funneling through the stem of the vintage hourglass; that slim Bosporus, shadowing each unity to Venus with rapt attention with all their aerials poking skyward—were seasoned by reinforced observers of varied biases and runes

While upon the ships, these batteries of flightless, attentive, earth-bound men, when not polishing decks, staffed them, stalking the pulchritudinous lady probes—the eclipsing subjects of their leak-like pungent-ness—from a very respectful distance

Venera-hounding ship roll call:

There is the *Cosmonaut Vladimir Komarov*

Here are the *Pavel Belyayev*
Georgi Dobrovolski
Academian Sergei Korolev
Academian Nikolai Pilyugin
Viktor Patsayev
Vladislav Volkov

Even a few converted merchant ships; the *Ristna*
Bezhitsa

And, of course, the *Cosmonaut*
Yuri Gagarin

Venera-6

She would not have replayed analog barks
during those so-long spans of affirming
as she sifted herself through near-vacuum

She was no mere flute-girl; there was no
time to gloat on embossed letters from men
being exchanged across the mailed ether

Crackles in vodka spoke a logos to
her which she obeyed as timely as
swole clocks obey beyond wound

Dipping into an atmosphere
she drifted calmly and
just as she was told to
she skimmed
wafted and then
unspooled herself
releasing the clutch
then just as St. Clare
had been so crushed
she too was trounced
by the ridiculous pressures
when she was still 18 kilo-
meters high, language left her—
untended and masticated amongst the clouds
within pulverized veils a crumpled cellophane

Bits of her siphoned undergrowth saturating all—
Sundered, she ceased aching as suspended rubble

she mushroomed; she spun and spun and spun and spun & as
an empire unstirred, emerged a sable-firmament around what

she had once been
she had been faith

Cinq Fragments

(i)

'Gamma ray bursts taste of venison,'
claimed their griefless madam,
          raising grooves to her drove

(ii)

She needed no windshield
No bugs splattered her

(iii)

The student crested the hot orb's shores—
holding her breath and taking an account—
          Brother sun was noticeably more present now

(iv)

Her grommets chinked
She barely blinked

(v)

The memoir genre was as off the table
as a gazelle's legs extend to the ground
          despite how suitably nonfictional we find them

Old Sheet Music

She knew nothing of doom in this woven depth
She hungered for not even an atom of yeast
          She was sanctimonious of groveling

Dark but far from formless; crystalized and fantastic
Hovering, beaming without pride or understudies
          Lights placed in the vault to divide everything

Dominating the night; a sovereignty bestowed on
a synthesis of presence. She stuck her trust into it
          She reckoned it to her merit

The muscles in her neck foretold eschatological victory,
She surged into radiance; she knifed; levitated as a saint
          Overtop the glens and ripples, a tide rolling on

She was dwarfed yet secured by incorruptible fabric
Her taste was not her own. She didn't merge with it;
          Her calloused dervish was quilted

Her wagon tracks overflowed with riches
She decked herself with all its bounties
          Similarly, she coated her masters

Her ribcage cracked at the doorway
Her lungs collapsed like a harpsicord
          She emitted splintering thrills

Mx. Freight Elevator not for General Public Use

had a boy-reporter typed columns about this gal like
    a dull county in Kansas he would have carefully
sifted her geography like a parading archeologist

he would have churned all her myths,
    her stories, romances, laws, and deaths,
photographed her assorted inhabitants—

directing their portraits in black & white
    vales with his vintage 35mm Pentax
recounting all varied individual interstices

of pneumatic effluvia & he'd have sketched
    their foibles with sanguine nipping rings and
the newsprint would have sold many copies but

this 'gal' wasn't taking passengers let alone
    some unruly cartoon Western correspondent
to her, a news cycle and a newt's cycle were

indistinguishable charred truckloads of the
    things she'd left behind; anyone trying to
sift her geography better write a will first

Venera-7 w/o frail gestures

Her yellow parachute detached   it slip-ungripped from a wrist
All her olives rolled away   the wet hyssop was misplaced

Its minty twigs shriveled   & the bullocks pointless
Her matchstick-style carrots   on blackened *khokhloma*

She was three kilos high   bouncing hard on the rocks
Her—the rocks—her—   rocks—more her—more rocks—

She was dashed against   the rocks and repaid in kind
Puzzling at 1% and then   within 23 minutes she was

Burned out of commission   churn-butter rendering zinc
Her receptivity to the   ascetical was cancelled out

Like a damn capitalist prank   she thoroughly undid herself
Her translations of photons   all went unpublished + unread

Her cleansing casementsall   collapsed & they crumbled
Roasted in the metal rains—   the hands of which—(if these

rains ever had hands)—were   so enormous & so uncongenial
that whatever lingered there   diminished 2-quick-primitively

Ragwort graph paper   numbed and racked

Dismissed   unwelcome

Unfathered   marred

Placement-vacant   basement-self-debasement

Faltered   wrecked

Garnished   wrecked

Wrecked   swept

Illus. 5

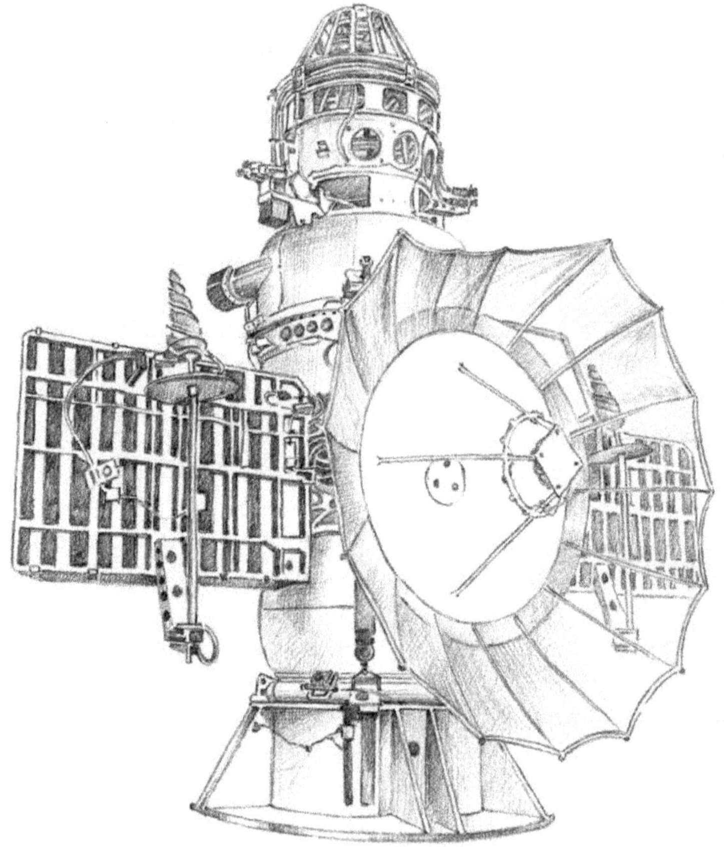

Venera-8

Witness our saint busty banking hard here again against nothingness (or nearly nothing)—bam-bam—thank you

Flitting this way and that fullsail proportionality—teaching

generating against the solar wind distinctions
assuredly tacking a barked distinction
back and forth
toward a

fiddleback speculum
which beckoned awash
while it pushed her back to a famous
smiling lemon which leans back which leans
away to pull her bedframe *in*
bream-trawling a heave-ho
upon her grace-hewn flitch

ultimately, she hooks, hooking herself
into a new consuetude
after having doggedly
fought for so long
through one univocal analogy
& for the other arrowhead Monet hay bale dunked in lavender
for so—for so long—and for not much; not much

later, she got to work—her descent touched down in the
monastery, and she itemized the curdled clouds ("1.1, 2.1, 3.1, 4.1,
5.2," etc.)—recording those persistent russet crannies ("one..."
etc.)—the linguistics in her immaterial ganglions negotiated a
spider-arm radius and settled into her computes; deftly, she
output-indexed the crust of a known/unknown woman's bulging
tan anatomy with her chastity, with care, without any
interruptions, bit-translating with ruler-sensitive variances—
spooling herself in to her, reeling the lady end-over-end in to her
as she stole the next science lesson from her paperclip-classmates
who melted like frost-spindles on a serf's window which hurt
which really truly hurt like bone bells before being read by anyone

Illus. 6

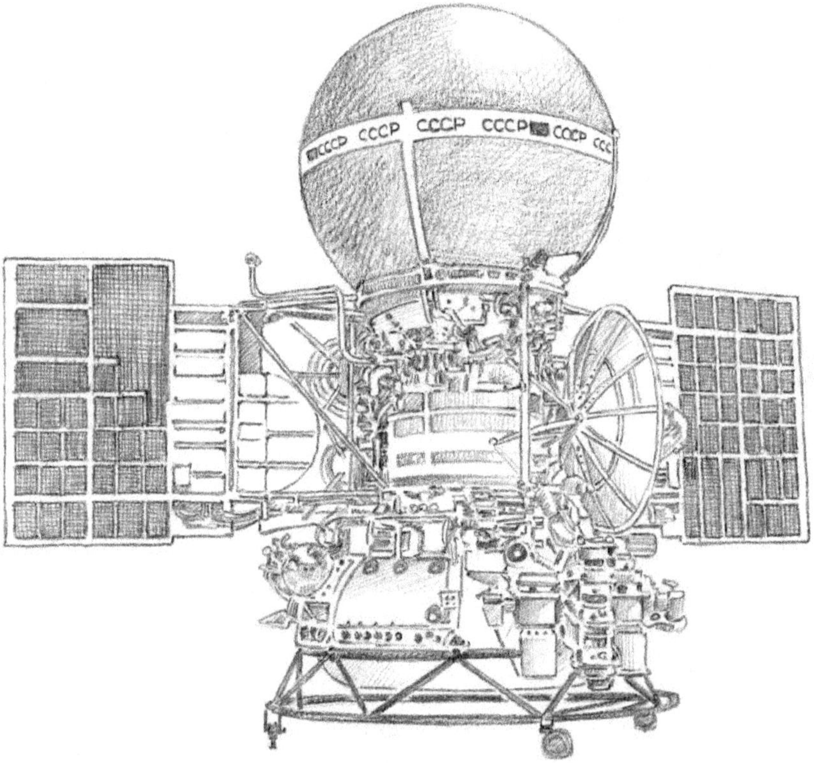

Birth Canal Weather Report Telegram

Ambition was as crystalized as a sermon
Squinting, she spotted Venusian lightning
which portended a grieving down the bend

A fair instrument, and she was not demeaned
Her tongue was coated with courage; her blouse
dipped in expulsion; her alignment undeniable

Circling something of such a greater mass
Her battery of bilious gadgets fed on data
with each lap around a striped telestic track:

lapping / tracking/ snapping
unimpaired and chugging
with a steam-puff carbon

She measured bi-static points, disjoining all
the gauze below (purported to be impenetrable
but for the shimmering electric spark-blades

which industrialized tensors and collarbones
in the rolling chasms of thunderhead-tipped
thousands) A rippling performance; bashful…

While coordinating these tasks she also
managed her mite's metallic nursing
Then she pressed a series of buckles &

unfettered her descent-vehicle-urchin
which unhanded from her like an egg:

toppling/ undulating/ snaking
unschooled and unlettered
with a child's persistence

she could donate pieces; calve herself off
until nothing remained but her epidermis

as she counted off the layers of clouds turning
the pages with a lick of her metal index finger:

Один…Два… Три

—as he fell of her
(or was it that they
gave birth to *each other*?)

at this crux in the timelage
a subarachnoid hemorrhage
introduced itself coyly

she rolled her pushrods, straining
she tapped her nonexistent legs
“It looks all downhill from here,”

#9 thought to herself
as lighting crashed
again, for emphasis:

.. - / .-.. --- --- -.- ... /
.- .-.. .-.. /
-.. --- .-- -. ....-.. .-.. /
..-. .-. --- -- / .... . .-. .

(this was the telegram)
(it came from lightning)

she transmitted against a use-ohm
voltage squared; an uncooperative
resistance-inductance flat-coned:

crashed   constants
currents   bunched
controls   snipped

off   she tapped again
she   messaged

waiting 4-a-sign

for
three times the boat whirred
and at the fourth to please
another's will the aft tipped in the air
the prow went down until the ocean
closed above our bones, wrote Dante and

Venus mused; told Venera
of her berth and churned
phlegm without such wit

The granary fused toy
soldiers in her hearth
on a twirling red spit

Venus, unbruised; closure
was her worth—burning—
demanded she submit

Venera-9 submitted
and, likewise, her tot
her birthed lost-self

stammered then one
last citation-resistor dielectric
shunted for three farads too, then signal full-stopped, end / end

ending

1975 Dresden Codex with Dual Carbs

Intertwining elongations
V-10's blue coupe could

set down on the busty curve
of a lip, dusting it so-mildly

as she loomed, an unlit bit-chine—
and she fell—silent. She fell silently

upon an ideology-free banquet laid
upon a mother too potent for most

A garden of scar-tissue-eskers—
Cicatrices earned; absconding

That frothy smile-wrinkle-plica. Its
wrinkles as adornments; as punishments

The hermit cab beheld an inlaid and
biscuit body; a sprig brimming with
beauties; each wholly unapproachable

This tanned woman's surface features—
All of which boasted women preachers;
The broadest provinces of her highlands:

Aphrodite / Ishtar / Lada (all Terras); and
Phoebe / Themis / Eistla (all Regios) and

There is: *Fossae / Fluctus / Farra*
There are: *Tholi / Lineae / Chasma*

There were desert-goddess dune-fields on her there;
& her craters: *Bodicea; Sacajawea; Maria Celeste…*

It is *Radunitsa Labyrinthus* premenopausal men
would most like to dance with and pull too close

(A Slavic goddess whose fetish will squirm
in both bodices) thin paragraphs of codices

If she wouldn't have a he, he'd ask
Chimon-mana Tessera instead she

a shapely swath of cross-polygonal-moraines
(& named for the Hopi goddess of the insane)

Our hermit-girl felt welcome; mother—
though imposing—was obliging—as
were her features, laid out like dishes

She let her pistons idle comfortingly
A fog studied itself from her louvers

None of that tanning was commercially
Sunk-into-skin (as it was in capitalist lots)

star-gazing: An Anonymous Venera

Ancient males deciphered patterns:
such as fish and scorpions; swords
and heroes—drawn from pin-pricks

Granted, the fine white tittle-hens they considered just that—
flecks in a drapery suspended above; higher than hawks
syllogize, tiny as dime tacks; motes haphazardly spilled

the brightest of them all was 'you-know-who'
lapsing-of-whomever's-counting-spin-results
she's a-lapping, in her tighter orbit, & traps us

every 584 days or so
and—as she does—
transposes herself—
flipping from an evening to a
morning eyelet—wink-wink-blink
winking and phasing / vertex-blinking her skein
admittedly, at times, it can be a little irritating, surveying

us, naturally enough, we construed her to be 2 heroines—
(the first one in the mornings, the other, the evenings) but
Pliny the Elder soon corrected us, just as naturally enough

A leading lady is at one with her
self, Pliny explained, So we sent
Venera, unhooked her a hi-deck

fleck, gyrating in the night ...
doing 'the hussle' working it

she became a diaphanous fleck
pinned, so no matter how she
stretched, nothing unplanned
was etched, nothing excepting
a bounty on the medial ledges

Venera-11 figures her figure

When this skater bustled in the night, she lost
footing on a rime and the night did something
to itself whereby she was overspread; secluded
in a darkness; nearly lost, thrusting & stretching

again stretching a stretched
gravel plat manuscript eel

but since this black space is
bound to blade back around
itself, all its delicate flecks

(except for her
an occasional angel
& maybe a comet or 2)

are thick buckling spheroids
all a-blaze & insides a maze

& at such a distance
as to affix all stance
as point-less asterisks

(at least without some help
from a fat catadioptric lens)

& she held it /in &
all was held in /her

another stitch in the pastiche; her needle working
beneath the dots—*a décolleté* of gussy organelles

Revolutions

This was how the solitarian
behooved a dexterous fleck

Yes, this is how, after much
steering and stretching she

did, in fact, find
that which within her
reach—reached

her

abode (which was
a sister-fleck 4 her;
a mother-brooch-pin!)

but it sure took lots of
stretching to get there

It is a good thing
that she wasn't
an agoraphobic—
going in & out
dangling/stich
-ing, no, this
skater kept
skep-wits
about her
and her
blades
down
cast

burn stage staccato

on her sound stage: ten
counterbalanced gyroscopes
she felt queasy she

became aloft with
the practiced focus of one
one who focuses

she became airborne
with the practiced focus of
one who practices

she consecrated
all into which she compassed
Dew blistered off tin

She waltzed barefoot on
the skin of thinnest water
furiously scribbling

It came down to this
this is what she came down to
down / this / her / to / rest

a / mess / her body: crosshatched
with toothpicks words solemnly
coughing up diastole propellants

Illus. 7

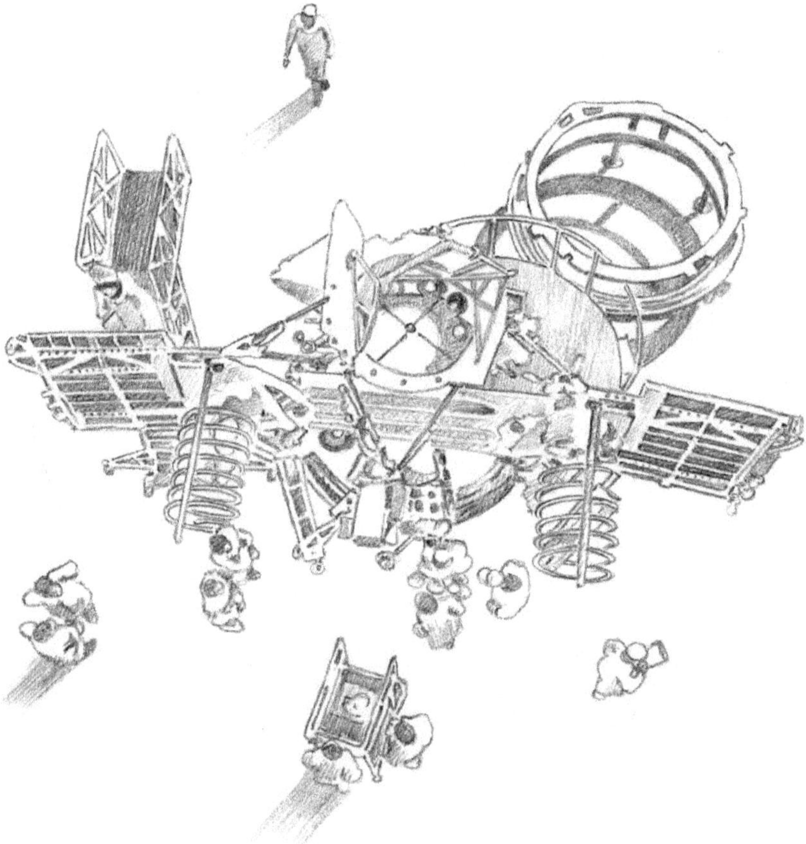

Venera-12 of happy memory

The maid took stock of
the interstellar medium
She was obsessed with
the gamma-ray bursts

She never tired of toying with her
lacy spectrometric measurements

She required two mid-
course corrections
one in September;
another in December

Those were the months
Those were the cults

One week later, she
divided herself as a host,
ejected her lander probe, and
continued on as a flight platform

Her probe emerged powerfully
not even crowning but zipping

This didn't bother her one bit
She relayed all that she found

Dividing oneself in the way that
she did was a becalming exercise
like switching out eyeglasses
for sunglasses once outdoors

A warrior-maid unperturbed by
this; a division of self which—
from all appearances—would
give an aproned man hysteria

ms. lonely planet

The rooms are less than luxurious. Indeed, there are no rooms as such. Instead, an assortment of squalid pup tents greets each visitor.

Pitched there haphazardly among the campsites nearest the inclines are numerous swirling corrosive mists of carbon dioxide. There, in the fog, one almost stumbles upon them—the tents; rows of them but none too straight. Bent. Tarpaulin triangles with lightweight poles thrust harshly through ringlets in the canvas and lightly scratching the surface of what is not an animal. Those poles will scrape away the gills from the fishless tourists—even the casual ones. (As if there are any other kind.) Those windmill minnows turn. That straw in the glass and no one to properly strain it. The cheeky hurricanes overpopulating the less attractive neighborhoods are as insufferable as the boulders masquerading as maître d's. They'll tire you out before you've escaped the train depot. On a positive note, however, they rarely demand a tip. They are ignoble.

Leave your gills at home or at least secured in your Samsonites® with their adorable little locks and charmingly undersized wheels since the surface temperature exceeds the highest setting on most household ovens by 400° or so and the atmospheric pressure is a crushing 90 bars, making the possibility of palms trees, coral, or even seraphs remote at best. A consular mocking at worst. It's hot.

One's luggage locks will be replaced by soldered teardrops before one resets one's wristwatch. And the wheels will drop out of their chassis like pregnant pits. There are no flies in the ointment because the flies are bits of ash. Torn muscle. Poorly crafted limericks. Jots. Invariably, they'll stick in your teeth. Bring floss. Recharge your razors. Fold your expectations and stick them in the teeth of anyone who asks you "Where did you get those shoes?"

The black and white photographs of the country's navel reveal something like the inside of a backyard grill that's been left on all night to cook itself to death, while the color photographs disclose yellowed tints from the smeary mustard sands. Smeared vindictively. It's as if she's cooked her own navel and served it to herself on a platter too hot to touch and then finger-painted on herself with a slightly rotted flaxen rouge. It's as if she's shoved a moth into a candle's flame and held it there, cauterizing her clenching.

It's all rather banal. Like mud-covered lanterns, the coastlines are ignored by the locals and for good reason. And it's warmer than a blast oven—if its climate was a kiln it would bust itself apart and spill open like a gourd. Hotter than an apogee furnace into which someone might cram an accidentally suffocated corpse—to remove any trace of it. To make it go away. To make bones be bygone. Cooking long after the springs are punched out. Cooking and cooking—roasting without rest.

So, consider sandals, a few smart linen outfits, a sun hat for the ladies or a rakish pith helmet for the gentlemen. Leave the wool blazers in Amiens. You won't miss them. Even the evenings are stifling. They turn one's crotch and armpits into soup. A soup without any seasoning and fit only for savages. And don't even think of inquiring about dry croutons. They're seldom available.

Indeed, the culinary options are limited. A rival travel guide warns: 'Unpacking, you'll find only a too-thick-hot-gelatin or overcooked magma on the room service list of options' (tactfully omitting the wrench-like mercury-filled bread sticks, despite their repetitive prominence on every menu). But another competitor notes: 'No grasses sprout, no breathing-into-nostrils-of-dust-balls was ever even contemplated; it's pristine' (mercurially pretermitting the inorganic fescue). Another hisses: 'Spare, terse, desiccated, and truly, on the whole, altogether uncompromising.'

'A life-changing destination for the suicidal,' wisecracks the last.

Accordingly, we recommend arranging one's exit visa prior to arrival. Don't rely on the expertise of the functionaries. The agents are irredeemable. It's almost as if custom and immigration forms haven't beset these primitives—or been invented—yet. One and one-half stars.

Illus. 8

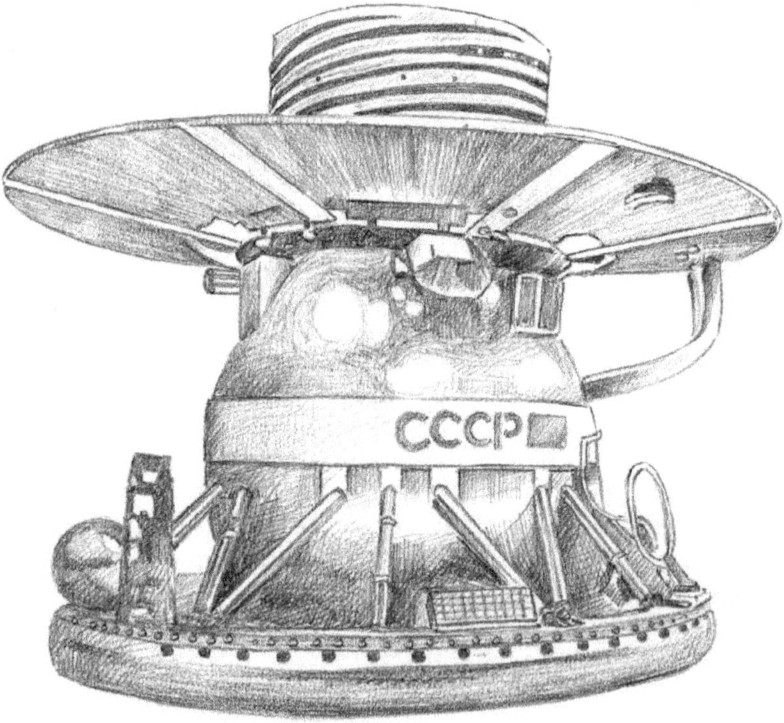

Venera-13

She surely felt light and airy
soaring above the nastiness in her
favored environment, recording,
savoring data, cavorting above

She was captaining herself
She set her keel
jammed her tiller
drawing precise circles
on the luxurious map with
herself—mapping proximally

herself captaining herself recover
and absorb sexy centrifugal forces

She absorbed no itch to descend
into the oven but when her orbit
decayed, that is what awaited her

And decay it did, inexorably,
as her type of orbit drift
nets always do—inset

No set fault be-smudged this oblate

this o captain she was a rooster
she was made of electricity and

When her cassette came
she'd have pulled anchor
and gone down with herself

Sinking to the bottom
Ploughing gimlet duets
sequestering her wonder

Venera-14

The hindmost probe summits on papules
A mountaineer held Cartesian carabiners
Eagles develop a cream-within-a-dream

She departed her bris on November 4 to
bravely meet the howls of a suffragist
in waiting for no one's ear, she creased
her ears and turned them below surfaces
listening a bad debt for operatic seismic

notes & parachuted and air-braked precisely
& when she planted herself on a hostile pan
she emitted 11 bouquets of crushed peonies

10 years later the Soviets would 'give up their dreams
for good'—Venetian and otherwise; they'd deliquesce

The Americans would question whether they ever had
'dreams for good' & at any rate, they'd say, 'so much
for communism' or 'so much for collectivism' & such
but they left impressions; they left their marks & much

more on a cutis, by Phoebe Regio's
eastern flank, on that unremarkable
basaltic a mountain-spiker-sojourn
persists like half-melted salt spilled
across a stovetop she's carved there

a handset of remainders of a cadet—
an octet with a span of her steps
in a place where gardening was

out of
the question

Unnamed—Unmarried—and Vital—she was V.15

neither fragile nor impeccable
repulsed by capitalist admirers

a few of her bones
were connected with
rather haphazard welds
but that wouldn't stop her

She'd gyrate in cursive
She'd deboss her map

She'd launch a corvid curtsey
Thoroughly smoothing all the
wrinkles out from her deltoids

She'd make a running jump
a cascading *tour en l'air* yes

she extolled justice
tracking the tract-less
the stars were her stairs

anything which was contrived
of material wants was cast off
Cyrillic symbols spilled from her
as the last marsupial marked-off

she left-justified her aerial to
ensure smooth transmissions
fully prepared and blessed,
she blinked out her elisions

She suppressed an erasure
Her chimney was a throat
Her triggers ran no gamut
Her streets beyond reproach

Venera-16

Radiantly attired and
making tracks for Fostal
buried just East of Cairo

Taking note of Canopus
her reference-point off
starboard, tasking her

caravan as it fanned
sand behind her trailer-hitch
A wake resembling testes

A starfish flower; her
pistil was erect; she
hacked out a switch-

back route through a
murderous slut-shaming
of deep-sea darkness

Much as this mosaic's
antler/tiara-ed princess
might have liked to,

she couldn't turn back
Nor would she have
liked to; she fancied

in statu viae as much
as the sweat glands
of what she had

left behind and
what *had* she left
behind but wetlands,

radio-friendly VIA,
& dressed herring?

Venera Monera

The lack of consensus of how to divide
Her phylum was blamed on informalities

Departures were not her strong suit
The airport runway threading away

Running up her hem—as a man's last
words to her—'a primitive pathogen'

Dividing itself in the small of a
Cup in which only ice remained

Roll was her co-pilot; a roll of
Peeling wallpaper, milk-soaked

Cheerios®, and oily clippings
No one would clip her wings

She'd conveniently misplace
Juvenile petitions to undulate

She took the throttle and
Yanked the altimeter fix

The acorn texture of a sweater too
Washed to offer a comfort to her

Neck and arcing away from arctic
Cabined blood of reindeer reminders

Missed itself from her phone
Without so much of a swipe

Illus. 9

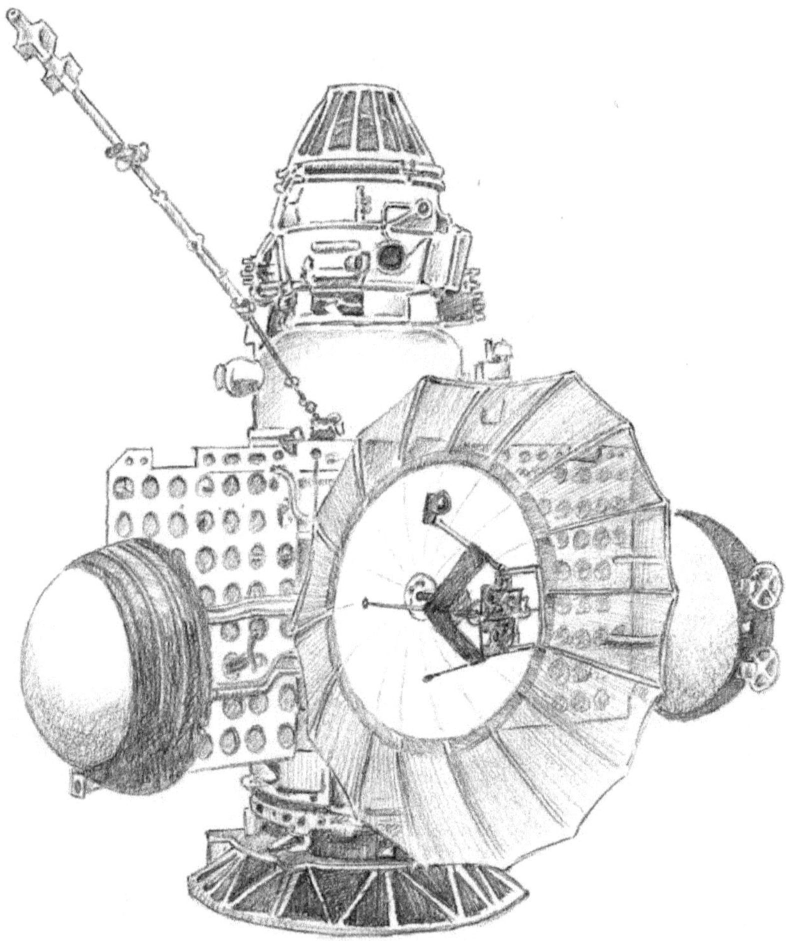

Zond-1 Distressed & Undressed

In April of 1964—
she set off calmly from Tyuratam

Initially, she enacted flawlessly
She would reach Venus's orbit;
the second Soviet probe to do so

She stood three meters tall with one-meter hips
She presented herself like a character out of
a Georges Méliès film as an enormous tin flower
opened out of belly button rivulets shamelessly

Her electronics bay was crowded with vacuum tubes,
papery glass troughs desperate for constant temperatures
and always at risk to overheating. Always ticklish.

A rocker-detector had been installed in her torso
just case she smote into something liquid. Just in case
there were liquids into which she might pilot and peck

(Though there weren't—
there wasn't even a tart
bit of rinse in a sink)

She malfunctioned following her
telemetry session and the last
contact with her was in late May

She attended the calamity ball in her cruise
phase: An almost-microscopic leak took
root slyly in a cracked sensor window

Consequently, and predictably:
Her electronics compartment
began to lose pressure; a replay of
her count-down but calamitously

numbers
became
progressively
dangerously
smaller
toward
three…
two…
and
one…
and
thus
panic
set
in

a tender-footed technician
mistimed a command to

her which she obeyed
honorably and tragically

'Tune your radio systems, Miss!'
which (of course) she did promptly

upon which something diminished
within her which wasn't a flower

but it was orange and petaled and
it pinned itself to her buttonholes

Zond-1 Debriefed

Within the still-rarefied atmosphere of
her electronics department, a corona
discharge blossomed; bloomed that May

it had conceived within her against her will
upon the command of a truly doltish swot

who had the thumbs of a rhinoceros and
vodka breath steeped with fried fig eggs

Still, her pin-thin corpse gestured
at home—speechless; inert, that
July—coasting, lugubrious, mute

But Chief Designer Sergei Korolev
was far from speechless he was out

-raged. Not only had the mission failed but
her little dirt-nap-fate presented an uncured
obstacle to his Orwellian renaming norms

retroactively revising all
women's names to outcomes

of changing feats to feasts
and fleets to her feet or
another way 'round

she couldn't be a *V*— as
she'd run aground too soon and

she couldn't be dubbed a *K*—
since she'd exited the campus oval

A new name
would be hers:
the first *Z*—

Zonds: co-eds who (allegedly)
had been designed to 'stress-
test components in deep space'

She had 'never wished
for a career anyway,' Sergei
Korolev assured everyone

He cleared his throat
when gazes dropped

'She preferred
domestic chores, men'

Whereupon the stale
roomful of man-eyes

rolled in unison plinking
lightly like Tropak dancers

The eyes were the chorus
to Sergei Korolev's

soliloquy and his frown
punctuated a shipwreck

Illus. 10

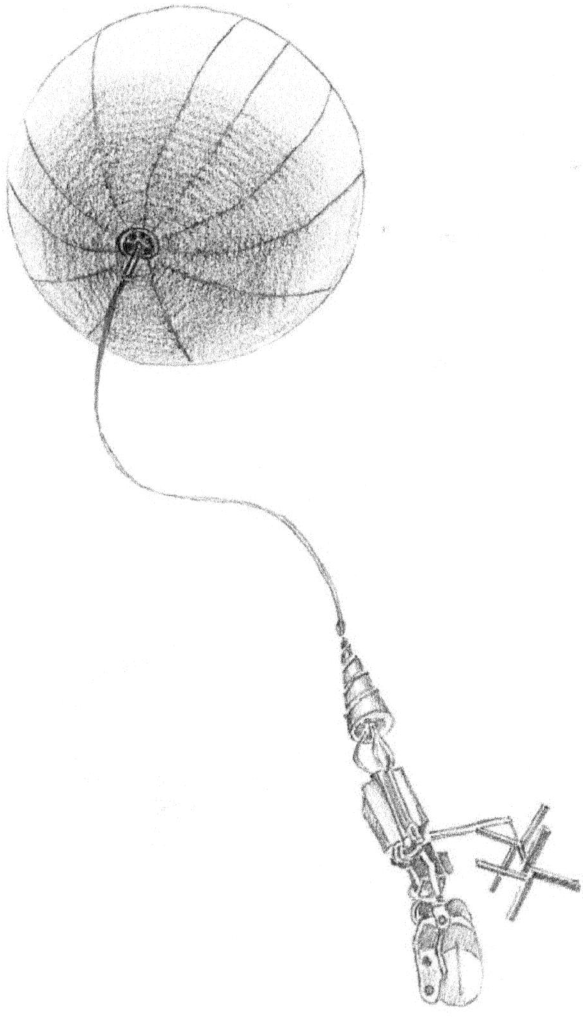

Vega-One-Two | Buckle-Their-Shoes

They were identical twin girls
& they debuted in in tandem
potently as twin thirsts often do

Each trekked to the morning
panjandrum and spit out a lander
and one instrumented balloon
each replete with helium stocks

The probes themselves didn't look back;
too anxious to rendezvous with some boy;
A solid boy-comet with a remarkable tail

What they'd spit carried no
cameras; conveyed no images
What they spit out were the
balloons—the aerostat probes

which twirled & brightened 53
kilos up for 46 hours & 60 hours
respectively—circling one-third
of their dignitary's circumference

What a pair they were; they
Embarked on a *pas de deux*

A trackless tumult cantered
Skimming the shingles high

They appliquéd the atmosphere
A rain of felicity applauded

The turbulence was ridiculous
The sulfur scanned sour to them

Those twin balloons puckered
Enjoying each other's company

Skating Backward @ Vertiginous Skate Land

They were two-of-a-kind
'That makes two-of-us,'
they sang simultaneously
They saddled up together
They were back in the
saddle again. They
were back-to-back
They felt welcomed back
B-b-back in the U.S.S.R.
It was good for them to be
back. It was good they had
each other's backs. They

made whorls of provender
Synapses set, they were
whorling around. They
weren't fuming around
They were dressed to
instill; they were women

drivers steering yet
none of their friends
sky-ed diamonds. They

were putting on a show
The show must go on—
and they were stealing it
They bewitched one another—
jocund and outspreading!
They were track-lapping
They lapped one another
They lapped up each other's
allegiances. They made up

a spectacle of themselves
over disinterested dunes
They were incorrigible

between 2 friends (16 candles) dropping drills

The 1st one awled her 2 bits
underneath some saddened
enraptured balloons as she
nestled in on the Mermaid
Plain north of Aphrodite
middled of a broken hilt
The 1st spuriously
bradawled her
brace before
touching down
quaintly crippling
it but the 2nd was
more cautious
and waited
until she
found purchase
then, upon auguring, her spade
perforated something—o!—&
she saw that she had discovered
something intentionally intricate
which smelled almost like anise:
anorthosite-troctolite & she pronounced it
"a finely
layered
igneous
intrusion
grey & rare" & she esteemed
& speckled a lunar highland
and her chestnut reminders
speckled both of them like
stenciled birthday sprinkles
above faint cries radiating from
what they'd plotted & battered though
"pain will not come forth from the ground"
& next they'd plat a pin-the-tail-on-the-donkey

Illus. 11

Her Tear Ducts Were Fuel Cells

She knit herself together
bracing for launch
She denounced gravity
Harbors repelled her
Her capacities were
unchecked by doubt

Surrender nauseated her
She would not be
reconciled to it
She was neither ripe
nor oozed, nor lusty

Rebellion sickened her. Her appetite for
credos was edacious. Her cloaks were
composed of avionics coated in jetsam

None of her bones contained cynicism
She hadn't a cynical bone in
her cylindrical body
Tenderness upset her
She afforded winks
Only upon herself

She embraced the
rods of discipline
Her coda ≠ caustic

She spurned cardigans
She repudiated shivers
Her orchestra ≠ frenetic

Modernity even in
moderation could never
hold her agglomerations

Divergence was not her kin
Salvation was not for her kind
Dreaming was not her crown

She wasn't the type for
lipstick and a wig. No,
nothing on her was painted

She was no 'bird'
No man's 'twist'

Despite her looks
her bright wings
and her gyrations
she was a prioress
cloistered in the abbey
called *Dancing-with-Myself*

Her mouth was not pink nor
was it as wet or small as she

was mouthless. Her uterus it was
seeded with gyroscopes and wires

Gluttony was not her bedfellow
Prophecy could not mislead her

She was properly led by
obedience, equations, &
a dram of nationalism

Her citadel was interiority
She praised the whirlwind
Her rectitude was seamless
Her seams were indefectible

She reveled in vulvar honor
She rechecked constants
She clasped humility tightly

She gave favors munificently
Mindful of a just future
She would find support

Her ears inclined to an instruction
Her bliss, abundant and conquered
Her innermost parts were cleaned

She charmed away worms
and named herself 'Aeronaut'

She could be medicinal
with self-mortification
She profited many
She cleansed us

She was a good soldier who
scorned a bulwark husband
Dipped in a honeycombed
wine, she disentangled knots

The Red French Balloon Proposal of 1983

In 1979 or so
Soviet-French
interplanetary
cooperation
(which boasted,
inter alia,
French scientific
tackle lugged
to Mars by the
USSR in 1971)
nearly hit
a new high
with an idea;
an event to
mark the 200th
anniversary of
Joseph-Michel &
Jacques-Étienne
Mongolfier's
1783 globe
aérostatique
balloon (fastened
with 1,800 buttons)
—a flight of which
had carried a sheep
named *Montauciel*
(climb to the sky)
in its basket—
by dropping a
huge sturdy red
commemorative
balloon staffed
with a 25-kg.
gondola of
scientific
paraphernalia
smack into the
brume of Venus

Jitter Bug Jitters

Before the dance
birds circled her
& a kick wheel

It wasn't clear if that orb
was luring her away or if
she lured seamstresses to her

Everyone would say, 'We all
thought so highly of your father.'
She'd not even shrug for now

her pilot light exon
sequenced uneasily

her flux was off her
syntax missing a bit

she was ½-a-bubble
off plumb; skewed

Predictably the boyfriends
drove her crazy checking
& rechecking her circuits

Pressing handmade things within
her abdomen she didn't like to have
pressed; every matrixed inch of her

They were driving her crazy
but soon she'd be doing
all the driving; she'd be

rag-rubbing her own
stain against her grain

Illus. 12

Venera + her man

His body: a vaguely-aged man with a Ph.D whose name was Iosif.
An ache at the temples was slurring his thoughts
A tent peg in both temples was truncating him; his mind—hovered
over screens in a room swarming with cigarettes. A room which had never been fresh; a room which felt lived-in because it was, as he traced a curved *'blip-blip-blip'*—her body was a pinpoint *'blip-blip-blip'*—across a trajectory

Venera's body: a steel & rivets rosebud. Hers felt lived-in, too.
Because it was, and she was a laughing new Jerusalem.
O she would unparallel any carceral archipelago frontier swiftly if
only something would be her venue before long. She (as one pinpoint) sought another pinpoint among many men

like Iosif, whose body was a man, rubbed his eyes. He missed his
wife and his daughters back at his flat
Bedraggled; he grimaced. He felt downtrodden. The long hours at
the control center were taking their toll while *this* trying child of a body of his; this *blip* on the screen was freeing herself from him more with each passing Stalin as children are wont to do. To Iosif, she was an effervescing candle in a contumacious gloom, overtly sure of herself; unguarded. If only she would allow him to over-take herself.

She vexed + bewildered him. This child took no naps. Unmysteriously she was
outlasting him. *This* child (whose hold was not stuffed with cherries and ink) *her* hold would not level an overflowing izba's attic with psalm books and hides
O beneath this child's orlop deck were Soviet expectations. This
child would excoriate Iosif mercilessly if he failed him-

self her rebuke would stick it to him with flat stickiness unknown
(except by the vinyl chair (on which he pebble-teetered) (and pig-iron-tottered))) squeaking defenestration loudly
Drumming his fingers and pulling on his cigarette; fussing; cussing becoming
softer and softer—while Venera was unshackled and gleeful as a new church key to the Urals

Rubor Fervor

See how her muscles ignite

She spits out the sugarcoated
Ready to capriole from a world
of green growing bandages

Her fuse pulls behind an orifice
sparking now inside her for
the count of three-two-one

Soon she would stretch what legs
she had; the chimney tops be-
coming ocelli; then cudgeled

What angels had taught her?
Above any mortal riptide
she struck doubters dead

She passed through scrapped gales
in our upper atmospheric layers
She struggled not; coined not

Ages before she'd be due for her
first overhaul, she'd be spent—
yet she had no ascension regrets

“She was a hot mass”

The ingredients for this sci-fi recipe—
as the apex-engineers scurry about—
in chronological-order of word-origin—are …

(1) 1-oz. *nougat;*
(2) 6mm *dross*; and a
(3) reliable *lye supply*

a lye supply free of vinegar
a dross funnel in measures

Her hands, steady on the spindle
laid out bread for her household

She'd spread herself; caught
upon rocks of eventfulness
like a dispassionate nougat
racked in a preheated oven

Had she been a poem of Tartars
she would've struck Pushkin's
flowery funeral garlands numb

but she wasn't she
was a candled cake
& amiable intelligence
to be baked at 820° for
twenty-five minutes or
until lightly browned
—and it wasn't artificial

this rocket ship was more than a
recipe she mixed more than beets

Upon Chiffon

She lived in the sky
The law was on her
like a colored robe
Her vocation was
stamped into her

Back on the launch pad
some teenage knucklehead
called her 'porn-star pretty'

She had neither
blushed nor
scowled then

& now she was above all that collection—
outside any contamination; inside silence
above presuppositions; beyond a sobriety
without any strife; despite concupiscence

hollowed out like a reed
forty honeybees buzzed
gladly within her cortex

She was out
of this world where lighted
covenants
were bright
by design
& where a
plan of
favors
had been
prepared
for her—
she radically
cantillated
the *Suscipe*

“The Guide of the Perplexed” (Vesta)

The concept of this pledge: It would have utilized
identical girls; too-ardent comrades who longed
for weddings and who would cherish one another

Their hearts would have
been sweet on each other
They would have been
each-other’s sweet-hearts;
heart-to-heart; they didn’t
wear their hearts on their
sheaves; they got to the
heart of it; their hearts
were set on it; they had
to depart, slyly satirizing
les enfants du paradis; our
twin-baby-scout-skippers
were galvanized for the journey
ready to egg on the wine-maker

But several months before their
oaths could be lettered the
‘some-how faraway’ lost out
& scrapped its heart-gear with it
So, instead of plans for resolute
cohorts conspiring and joined
(‘some-how *joined-at-the-hip*’)
bud-eared bairns would spider
from their undersides and the 2
girls would then abandon them to
inspect some interesting asteroids

Yet even this plan was abandoned altogether—
when communism was abandoned all together

the pair lost heart
they were no longer whole
hearted but started being
hole-hearted, etc., etc., etc.

Illus. 13

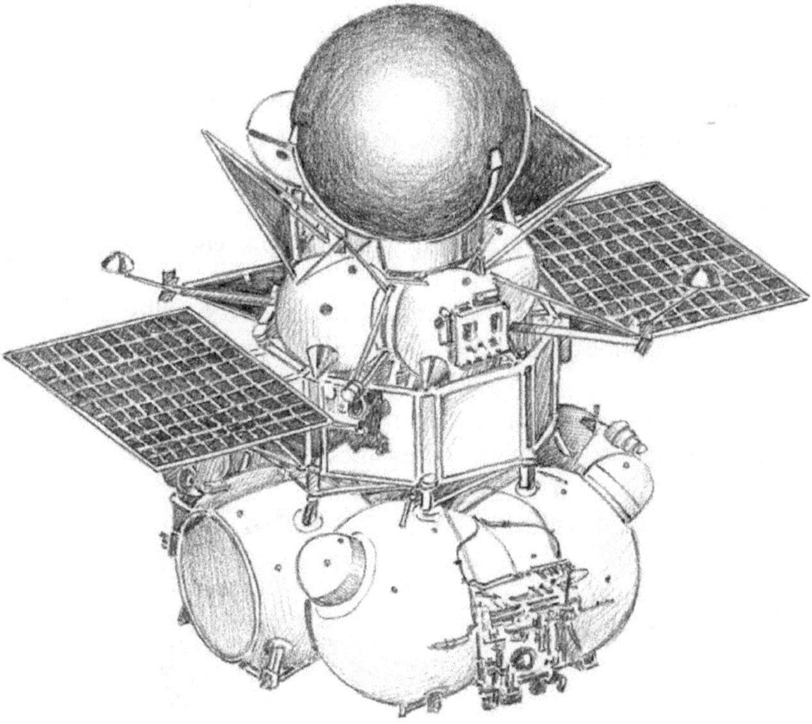

Mindful (*Refrain)*

Notice: Peculiar pebbles on her embonpoint in a mind's eye
Observe: Discrepancies; plump crags; a set—mindful of one

another—on her solar transit-waist; circular, not elliptical
She counter-turns so deliberately that days outstretch years

A day *outlasts* a year on her; she gloats a nonpareil wit
and orbits with the confidence of a classical education

Ladies planted there frozen-hot, forever stationary
and—in one sense—never again to *brisé* a path-curl

But in another sense, each of them will still spin and circuit
with an adhesion; a synchronicity to their sovereign; firmly

matched to wheel, each of them is seated where they'll stay—
their revolutions quieted, their itchings calmed and recumbent

transfixed to an authoritative Damascus meant to be their home
interpreting their ladyship's core—these ladyships themselves

Sing: a potency recalled—

O tell of their trips,
O sing of their grace
Whose robes were of steel,
whose canopies space

No charioteers steered them,
no rust ever formed
Quick were their paths
on the cusps of the storms *(Repeat)*

Illus. 14

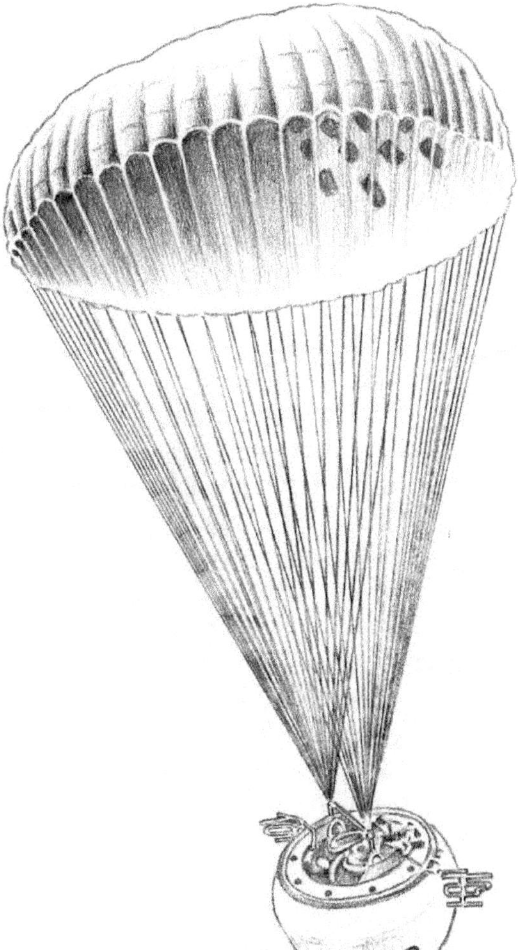

Burnt Offerings

Smooth
shining silver domes
cresting yellow winds
stained like men's teeth
Round mirrored ones
blest by Soviet nuns
whistling with them
A psalm maskil fancies
yellows like refiners' fire
Lay on fullers' soap
Noetic recitations
Celibate chants
Full of sap
Strong as wild oxen
Repetitions and soundings
Sanctifications: roundings
The music of the spheres
by domes upon a sphere
Carved-in and rooted
Solemn there; stay
No adversary shouts their names
The gale screams at someone else
Soft agent of tarnished
silver much vouchsafed
A people without power who
made their home in the rocks

Sternums like flint
flocks racing
Raisin-curtseys
grasp prayer
Palms waving
raising
Rest, encrusted,
undefiled there:
Pilgrims,
Thrive!

Pushkin's Decorations: Letters in & by him (2023)

near midday Pushkin's bones found their hour they poked themselves a brackeny window; turned turf, escaping the courts' silage, chalk-scratching buttercups to emerge a being with which they had become   radically unfamiliar   Pushkin's own osseous

matter was done temporizing and resting the being that the world had become in the 184 years since they'd wrapped sinews; a Venus-shaped girl mouthing Russian slang ignored everything but those bones were something why   a vague thing could easily go

unnoticed in the oil-soaked soil those bones had overlooked the Lenin-to-Gorbachev-chapter; some things take too long to list; now sniffing, she—this girl readily   apprehended that she could connect a bronzed bog-like trashed latch   the bones could

sniff a sharp whiff: Putin's chest; were it on horseback she might not have sniffed it & so sunken was it, cluttered with broken hasps, it cooled recognitions & considered yoking our adolescent girl's fingernails scrimming away laced roots and a rectangle exchequer

parting tycoon worm segments for she had   revenues she had a trophy and the crowns imparted a patience swelling her chest—she disinterred a treasure chest she exhumed that which she possessed what-was-needed she possessed   her possessions well

beyond her busybody rivals' riches she possessed that-which-she possessed a 'for the sake-of-which' to intone paired rhymed tercet-lines   and so unbury those bones symphonically to the initial off-key chords   of her   in this new sighing

> *sigh* … (tuning)
> *sigh* … (gathering steam)

then pneumatically (pumping)
and the near-perfect pitch (peeping)

of the unschooled   notable singing thus:

Her head is bowed

Her heartbeat skips

A light smile flutters
upon her lips

tuned as she did to the bones which almost made   the bones smile; she was a princess, an adolescent as strong as a planet with rocket adzes   with which to mate those buried verses   she suppressed carnality   she tipped her trowel   to sing more verses

small, majestic, and unwed, she yielded his letters & his sonnets she wielded his songs & his bullet-hole bonnets as woodland beasts padding the leaves; thick as affronts   turned their ears heeding her gallantry   & exposed their necks to her rich jams

Postlude Pads

Forceful mind debris
Those not-shy taproots

of ours still stubbornly
sticking to rattling flesh

doggedly insisting on
faithfulness 2 foundations

& their own contributions
to her dearly won influence

untamed ferments squeal
stubbornly creating tiny

vortices for the winds
to notice—a scherzo

melody

Such
    stubborn
        poets;
            trinkets
                saluting
                    upon

            Frisky Venus
            Precarious Venus

spot-welded in place by lava-hot winds
on the rocky, untouched, neural plenum
There, they had assembled themselves

at the dotted-lines expiries of their
junkets and in the end, neither Venus

nor her cinture-of-dunes nor
her flesh-of-sharp-canyons
were altogether unmoved by

them; Now their features
complemented one another;
complimented each other

The landing crafts—
a coenobia in a
cenobium's umbra

linked ladies leasing
a tower and a winepress
from their terce-host

So too
                on   Hoary Venus
                             Breathless Venus

If one listens carefully,
one can almost hear them
voice sext-vespers together

These round sectioned Hebrew
vigils tucked in their vestries—
here, there, and everywhere—

                like the boy who wanted freckles
                so much that he metastasized
                an acne with a magic marker

                and went to school, proud
                of his red-dotted handiwork
                his face a speckled quail egg

                his sister had been one to tell
                him he looked foolish but she
                wouldn't; it'd quash his smile

those ‘freckles’ were his own
and she left them there as he
had made them for what joy

he betook in their arrangement
as she beheld him less as a sister
might, than as a mother would

So too
on   Maternal Venus
                      Fetching Venus

Who tattooed *her* brow with those women-sparks?

Lovely lopsided cairn coins
speckling a created compline

Like owls in the wilderness
Little lamps in the waste places

Pale flickers / warm valor, there:

No megaliths shade them and
assuredly, He is far from displeased

by our relics’ humble contributions to their
own collective velocities ‘round that sphere

that spotted yellowed-vase as
smokeless: ashes—ashes
which maintain a stasis

unconsuming—hand-in-hand—gathered—initiated

in close propinquity to the landscape where to
gather—to send / to fend / they to—
                      gether—wedding;
                      treading; go now
                      and blend

Closing Argument

The Soviets went to Venus, wisely sending surrogates, given the distances involved. They transported their material culture—spoked with gently engineered receptors—there; a place where one would be crushed by a pressure equivalent to being half a mile underwater boiling furiously away at a lead-melting 850° F (though Tennyson imagined Venus "a world of never fading flowers"[1] and Bradbury evoked her "cheese-colored leaves" [2]).

They—we—went to that groaning globe. We aimed silvery specters at a destination where, without the distractors of sin or suffering, the vapor of the divine might congeal, despite (or perhaps aided by) the intense heat. Those probes were eyepieces. They were each a flame-powered girlish gorgeousness that we shot into the sky in order to see a beauty otherwise too dim. To see beauty; to wonder, is itself beautiful. The Venus probes necessarily functioned as extensions of our interiors; our sensory apparatus. To extend our perception of a creation farther than ever before—far into it—was both noble and pleasing.

Consider those sparkling silvery artifacts we sent skyward. They have an aesthetic. What we and the Soviets did—and how we did it—was spectacular. If we sowed something which still glimmers on Venus, what was it? Competition? Conflict? A germ of consolation? A mere collecting of data?[3] Or something more?

We were not the makers of the planetary spheres, but we crafted the probes to Venus; we set them a-blazing. They obliged. They steamed across a created fabric; a designed quilt. Then they cloistered themselves on Venus like medieval nuns.

Today, too often, we cast our eyes downward, onto screens. Medieval thinkers looked up. They gazed heavenward and saw the quilted-ness of it all. C.S. Lewis explained this aspect of the medieval mind and how it conceived of the qualities of stars:

---

[1]Alfred Tennyson, *Locksley Hall Sixty Years After* (1886).
[2]Ray Bradbury, *All Summer in a Day* (1950).
[3]*See Book of Psalms* 90:17 ("proper for us the work of our hands—O prosper the work of our hands!").

> The relation between the Intelligence of a sphere and the sphere itself as a physical object was variously conceived.... Hence Donne, speaking of our own bodies, can say 'We are the intelligences, they the spheare'.
>
> Later, the Scholastics thought differently. 'We confess with the sacred writers', says Albertus Magnus, 'that the heavens have not souls and are not animals if the word soul is taken in its strict sense. But if we wish to bring the scientists (*philosophos*) into agreement with the sacred writers, we can say that there are certain Intelligences in the spheres ... and they are called the souls of the spheres...[4]

In his cosmic trilogy (a space trilogy, in fact), Lewis claimed that one could perceive the etchings of male and female far beyond the rim of earth, occupying all of that sparkling vastness.[5]

Not one Venera (nor any Zond) had a sexed body in the vulgar sense. This is not simply a question of testes and phalluses and vulvas. Neither is it a question of X or Y secondary chromosomes. Nor hormones. Nor preferences. Nor desires. But something much more deeply embedded in the cosmos itself. In the subatomic.

To assert that certain truths are given to us, and not decided by us, is not to say that nastier individuals may impose their preferences on others. It is not to say that the majority may constrains the lesser to its own views and its own prejudices. Democracy in its absolute form is a tyranny and it is fascist. We ought not to vote on these things, nor delegate them, either. It is simply to say that certain realities are gifted to us by something which is not us.

Most moderns assume that the universe is mostly empty and meaningless; devoid of male and female; that we will not encounter sexes in neighboring galaxies. Moderns assume a nonbinary cosmos. But Lewis claimed that sex was not a mere marker in social cultures, nor a convenient pattern at the zoo, but that it was observable even in geology. In strata. Or clouds. Indeed, the entire

---

[4]C.S. LEWIS, THE DISCARDED IMAGE 115 (1964).

[5]His "space trilogy" is sometimes referred to as the "cosmic trilogy." C.S. LEWIS, OUT OF THE SILENT PLANET (1938); C.S. LEWIS, PERELANDRA (1943); C.S. LEWIS, THAT HIDEOUS STRENGTH (1945).

universe is suffused with two sexes, even in objects and artifacts that are seemingly non-sexed. The imprinting was not merely pre-Columbian; but pre-human. Pre-us.

Saint Francis, also a medievalist, acknowledged this.[6] No sailor, no engineer, can seriously doubt that ships are women.[7]

The womanly-ship tradition relates to the sensibility that a construction of wooden ribs which shields its inhabitants and transmits a mission across time and space toward a preconceived destination through the hazards of storms and tides is akin to a mother who guides and protects her crew. A Saint Mary. The Soviet probes were empty of men or women. Their wombs had wires. Their ribs contained only switches. They lacked crews, except for the men (mostly men) staffing their navigations. And their missions were both scientific and nationalistic. Not solely maternalistic. After all, we made them. We were their creators; we crafted those probes to do what we willed them to do.

But perhaps those probes *were* womanly. Perhaps there is sex—or sexes—in space. Perhaps our journey through the ether is not preordained but preprogrammed—if and to the extent that we would listen to a voice that speaks to us in the silence of space. If rocket scientists might pray. If we might listen. And glance up.

---

[6]*See* G.K. CHESTERON, SAINT FRANCIS OF ASSISI 91 (1924) (noting St. Francis's "sense of sex in inanimate things"—masculine winds, manly fires, ladylike waters, feminine spheres, etc.).

[7] "Ship" is derived from the Latin *navis*; a feminine noun.

Acknowledgements

Credit is extended to the editors of the publications where these poems (or earlier versions of them) first appeared:

"Her Tear Ducts Were Fuel Cells" and "The Red French Balloon Proposal of 1983" (as "The Red French Balloon Proposal") in THE WRITE LAUNCH (Feb. 2020)

"Rubor Fervor" (as "Ignition") in TAJ MAHAL REVIEW (June 2020)

"Potency Recalled" in UTOPIA SCIENCE FICTION (Aug. 2020)

"V-3" in 365 TOMORROWS (Aug. 20, 2020)

"Since," "Geography Lesson," and "Kosmos-21" in SCARLET LEAF REVIEW (Nov. 2020)

"Runway Model Rocketry," (as "Model Rocketry") and "Venera-7 w/o frail gestures" (as "without frail gestures") in AROMATICA POETICA (Dec. 2, 2020)

"Soviet Scientists *Canto 1*: Konstantin Tsiolkovsky," (as "Soviet Rocket Scientists: *Canto 1*: Konstantin Tsiolkovsky"); "Soviet Scientists *Canto 2:* Yuriy Vasilievich Kondratyuk," (as "Soviet Rocket Scientists *Canto 2:* Yuriy Vasilievich Kondratyuk"); "Soviet Scientists *Canto 3*: Gavriil Adrianovich Tikhov," (as "Soviet Rocket Scientists *Canto 3:* Gavriil Adrianovich Tikhov"); and "Soviet Scientists *Canto 3.5*: Tikhov in Awkward Rhyme" (as "Soviet Rocket Scientists *Canto 3.5*: Tikhov in Awkward Rhyme"), in THE SHOWBEAR FAMILY CIRCUS (Jan. 4-8, 2021)

"Postlude Pads" (as "Venetian Landing Crafts: A Survey") and "Burnt Offerings" in AMETHYST REVIEW (Jan. 31, 2020; Mar. 20, 2021)

"ms. lonely planet" in RUE SCRIBE (March 21, 2021) (republish-ed by 365 TOMORROWS (March 29, 2021))

"A Spaceship Named Rapture" in DREAMS & NIGHTMARES (May 2021)

"Old Sheet Music" in PROVOKE: A BACKLASH JOURNAL (Summer 2021)

"Burnt Birds and Flowers" in THE MARTIAN WAVE (Sept. 2021)

Table of Probes

Launch Date	Spacecraft/Type	Outcome
02/04/1961	Tyzahely Sputnik/*Impactor* (a/k/a IVA #1)	Launch failed
02/12/1961	Venera 1/*Impactor* (a/k/a IVA #2)	Spacecraft failed; flyby without data
08/25/1962	2MV-1 No. 1/*Lander* (a/k/a Sputnik 19)	Failed to exit Earth's orbit
09/01/1962	2MV-1 No. 2/*Lander*	Launch failed (*re:* upper stage fuel valve)
09/12/1962	2MV-2 No. 1/*Flyby*	Launch failed (*re*: bubbles in 4th stage fuel)
11/21/1963	Kosmos 21/*Unknown* (a/k/a Cosmos 21)	Launch failed
02/19/1964	3MV-1 No. 2/*Flyby*	Launch failed (*re:* oxidizer leak)
03/27/1964	Kosmos 27/*Flyby-Lander* (a/k/a 3MV-1 No. 3)	Launch failed (*re:* altitude control)
04/02/1964	Zond 1/*Flyby-Lander*	Spacecraft failed (*re:* electronics short)
11/12/1965	Venera 2/*Flyby* (a/k/a Sputnik 20)	Spacecraft failed

11/16/1965	Venera 3/*Lander*	Spacecraft failed
Launch Date	Spacecraft/*Type*	Outcome
11/23/1965	Kosmos 96/*Flyby*	Launch failed (*re:* 3rd stage explosion)
06/12/1967	Venera 4/*Atmospheric*	Success
06/17/1967	Kosmos 167/*Lander* (a/k/a 4V-1 No. 311)	Launch failed
01/04/1969	Venera 5/*Atmospheric*	Success
01/10/1969	Venera 6/*Atmospheric*	Success
08/17/1970	Venera 7/*Lander*	Landed but rolled (first "soft" landing)
08/22/1970	Kosmos 359/*Lander*	Launch failed
03/27/1972	Venera 8/*Lander*	Success
03/31/1972	Kosmos 482/*Lander*	Launch failed
06/08/1975	Venera 9/*Orbital-Lander*	Success (took images of the surface)
06/14/1975	Venera 10/*Orbital-Lander*	Success
09/09/1978	Venera 11/*Flyby-Lander* (a/k/a 4V-1 No. 360)	Partial success with lander instrument failures

09/14/1978	Venera 12/*Flyby-Lander*	Partial success with lander camera failures
Launch Date	Spacecraft/*Type*	Outcome
10/31/1981	Venera 13/*Flyby-Lander*	Success (holds record of 127 minutes of operational existence on the surface)
11/04/1981	Venera 14/*Flyby-Lander*	Success
06/02/1983	Venera 15/*Orbiter*	Success (orbited until July 1984)
06/07/1983	Venera 16/*Orbiter*	Success (also orbited until July 1984)
12/15/1984	Vega 1/*Flyby-Atmospheric* (a/k/a 5VK No. 901)	Partial success
12/21/1984	Vega 2/*Flyby-Atmospheric*	Success
n/a 1994 (cancelled)	Vesta/*Orbiter-Lander*	n/a
n/a (2026?) (proposal only)	Venera D/*Orbiter-Lander*	n/a

Partial Bibliography

BRIAN HARVEY, RUSSIAN PLANETARY EXPLORATION: HISTORY (2007) (New York, NY: Springer Praxis Books)

BRIAN HARVEY AND OLGA ZAKUTNYAYA, RUSSIAN SPACE PROBES (2011) (New York, NY: Springer Praxis Books)

WESLEY T. HUNTRESS JR. AND MIKHAIL YA MAROV, SOVIET ROBOTS IN THE SOLAR SYSTEM MISSION TECHNOLOGIES AND DISCOVERIES (2011) (New York, NY: Springer-Praxis Books)

Don P. Mitchell, *Plumbing the Atmosphere of Venus* (2003) available at http://mentallandscape.com/V_Lavochkin1.htm

ALEXANDER PUSHKIN, YVGENY ONEGIN (1823-31) (Anthony Briggs, trans., London: Pushkin Press, 2016)

ASIF A. SIDDIQI, BEYOND EARTH: A CHRONICLE OF DEEP SPACE EXPLORATION, 1958-2016 (2nd ed. 2018) (Washington, DC: National Aeronautics and Space Exploration)

Venera-D: Expanding Our Horizon of Terrestrial Planet Climate and Geology Through the Comprehensive Exploration of Venus (2019) (Phrase II Report of the Venera-D Joint Science Definition Team), available at https://www.lpi.usra.edu/vexag /reports/Venera-DPhaseIIFinalReport.pdf

About the Author & the Illustrators

Thomas E. Simmons is a lawyer and professor at the University of South Dakota's Knudson School of Law. He teaches courses such as Estate Planning and Professional Responsibility. Most of his scholarship considers inheritance and trust law, but he also composes literary criticism, theological commentary, film analyses, and history. He is an academic fellow of the American College of Trust and Estate Counsel (ACTEC), a lifetime member of the American Society for Legal History (ASLH), and an Associate Justice of the Rosebud Sioux Tribe Supreme Court. Previously, he authored *Loose-Leaf Tod Browning Encyclopedia* and *S is for Sentence,* both published by Cyberwit.

Simmons fretted over the history of the Soviet scientific missions to Venus with something approaching a low-grade obsession for several years. Carefully mapping the trajectory of each Venetian spacecraft from the USSR, he has reconstructed, in verse, their successes and the failures, as well as those mission outcomes which have been obscured with propaganda and falsehoods. This collection is a product of his incessant pining and preoccupation.

###

Yasemin Arkun, of Istanbul, Turkey, is the creator of the interior illustrations. She is a professional freelance visual artist. After graduating with a degree in architecture, she worked as a 3-D visualization artist and designer in architectural offices and as a freelancer. Despite her busy schedule, she kept pursuing her career as a painter and a visual artist. Since 2017, she has been a full-time freelance artist. She uses various mediums, such as graphite, watercolor, acrylic, and oil. Besides portrait commissions and various works, she has illustrated several children's books.

Paul Peterson, of Sturgis, South Dakota, is the creator of the cover image, *Aeromotor Grey Painting* (acrylic, 10"x15") whose mechanical whirring sounds rather Venera-esque. When he is not painting in his studio, he can be found playing guitar at various venues. See paulpetersonart.com.

www.ingramcontent.com/pod-product-compliance
Lightning Source LLC
Chambersburg PA
CBHW020857160426
43192CB00007B/963